T0147731

RELATING
TO THE
TITHE
According to the Word

STEPHEN HERVEY

WESTBOW
PRESS®
A DIVISION OF THOMAS NELSON
& ZONDERVAN

Copyright © 2020 Stephen Hervey.

All rights reserved. No part of this book may be used or reproduced by any means, graphic, electronic, or mechanical, including photocopying, recording, taping or by any information storage retrieval system without the written permission of the author except in the case of brief quotations embodied in critical articles and reviews.

WestBow Press books may be ordered through booksellers or by contacting:

WestBow Press
A Division of Thomas Nelson & Zondervan
1663 Liberty Drive
Bloomington, IN 47403
www.westbowpress.com
1 (866) 928-1240

Because of the dynamic nature of the Internet, any web addresses or links contained in this book may have changed since publication and may no longer be valid. The views expressed in this work are solely those of the author and do not necessarily reflect the views of the publisher, and the publisher hereby disclaims any responsibility for them.

Any people depicted in stock imagery provided by Getty Images are models, and such images are being used for illustrative purposes only.
Certain stock imagery © Getty Images.

Scripture taken from the New King James Version®. Copyright © 1982 by Thomas Nelson. Used by permission. All rights reserved.

ISBN: 978-1-9736-7301-9 (sc)
ISBN: 978-1-9736-7300-2 (e)

Print information available on the last page.

WestBow Press rev. date: 09/17/2020

This book is dedicated to my daughters, Rachel and Hannah, who are a great blessing to me from God. I thank Almighty God for the grace and gift that He has given me to glorify Him and to minister to others. I pray that this book will be a blessing for those who are seeking the truth.

"I will say of the Lord, He is my refuge and my fortress;
My God, in Him I will trust. (Psalm 91:2)

Preach the Word! Be ready in season and out of season.
Convince, rebuke, exhort, with all longsuffering and teaching.
—2 Timothy 4:2

To preach the Word, it must be according to the Word.

CONTENTS

PREFACE

One of the most popular topics by many preachers today is the subject of tithing. One of the first things a novice will learn if he or she does not already know is that the word *tithe* means a tenth. In many churches it is expected of members to pay a tithe of their income to the church plus give additional offerings besides the tithe. It is ironic how tithing is frequently mentioned by many and is also one of the most misunderstood subjects of the Bible. It is hard to watch a television evangelist without hearing the word *tithe* at some time during the program. The doctrine of tithing money has been dogmatically taught by many and has been unquestionably accepted by many. One of the iterative warnings within the Bible is that many teaching many is not a factor for creditability.

One of the primary purposes for this book is to address the doctrine of tithing in many of the churches of God. I certainly advocate members supporting church ministries but not by mandating monetary tithes. Church members have the right to freely give whatever amount they choose in supporting the work of God. Mandating monetary tithing was not the policy implemented by Jesus, the head of the body. Ministers are abusing authority when they coerce or mislead people to pay monetary tithes without the consent of our Chief Shepherd. Many are being swindled because of a lack of understanding of what the Word says about tithing.

Hosea 4:6 says, "My people are destroyed for lack of knowledge." A lack of knowledge of God's Word can be destructive, and one of the subjects that the Word talks about is tithing. Every Bible believer should believe what the Word says about tithing, and all believers should benefit from knowing the truth about tithing and godly giving. Second Peter 1:2–4 says,

Grace and peace be multiplied to you in the knowledge of God and of Jesus our Lord, as His divine power has given us all things that pertain to life and godliness, through the knowledge of Him who called us by glory and virtue, by which have been given to us exceedingly great and precious promises, that through these you may be partakers of the divine nature, having escaped the corruption that is in the world through lust.

Without Partiality

James 2:1 says, "My brethren, do not hold the faith of our Lord Jesus Christ the Lord of glory, with partiality." First Timothy 5:21 says, "I charge you before God and the Lord Jesus Christ and the elect angels that you observe these things without prejudice, do nothing with partiality." Partiality is incompleteness by not looking at all the facts. James 3:17 says, "But the wisdom that is from above is first pure, then peaceable, gentle, willing to yield, full of mercy and good fruits, without partiality, and without hypocrisy." The Word affirms that there is no partiality with God (Eph. 6:9, Acts 10:34).

Deuteronomy 1:1 says, "You shall not show partiality in judgment." We should be careful to not be prejudiced, which means to prejudge or judge before getting all the facts. Being biased can involve coming to a conclusion before having adequate knowledge, which is also unfairness or injustice and is contrary to the wisdom of God. The equivocal comments by many preachers on tithing often involve partial truth. Partiality is being blind to the whole truth, and when it comes to the truth about tithing, it seems that most people have only heard about a tithe of the truth.

Prove all Things

The book of Acts records how Paul and Silas went to Berea into the synagogue of the Jews to preach the Word, which the members there received with eagerness. Acts 17:11 says that they "searched the Scriptures daily to find out whether these things were so." If Paul had preached on tithing the way most preachers do today, those at Berea would have found out from searching the scriptures that what many teach on tithing does not concur with the Word of God.

Most people are not aware of the fact that there are two types of tithing. The two types of tithing can be categorized as biblical and nonbiblical tithing. There is tithing according to the Word of God, and there is tithing according to the commandments of men. First Thessalonians 5:21 says, "Test (prove) all things hold fast what is good." The old and new covenants talk about tithing, but no one can prove that the tithing of money is a scriptural requirement.

INTRODUCTION

Relating to the Tithe
According to the Word

S tephen grew up in a military family where he participated in a variety of sports and excelled in both football and wrestling. After graduating high school, he entered Lock Haven University, PA on a wrestling scholarship. Two years later Stephen decided to join the USA Marine Corp where he earned a spot on the Greco Roman Wrestling Team. While in the Marines, Stephen learned about the World Wide Church of God, (WWCOG) and eventually embraced and joined the faith.

Believers of the WWCOG faith conscientiously refuse to bear arms or to follow military authority. Stephen completed his tour of duty and received an Honorable Discharge From The USA Marine Corp. It was through the WWCOG that Stephen met his future wife Sarah. They married and settled in Newport News, Virginia eventually starting a family and raising two girls, Rachel and Hannah, the center of their lives.

Over the years, Stephen witnessed issues in the Church of God which resulted in at least one split within their Church. The emphasis on tithing was becoming more uncomfortable both in the Church and sadly within his marriage. Stephen realized that a number of parishioners were being subjected to pressure, manipulation, and even coercion. He was quick to state that members should most definitely financially support their churches, but was opposed to the over emphasis on tithing.

Pressure over tithing increased to the point that his wife left him and his pastor banned him from their church. Meanwhile, a mysterious pain in Stephen's joints was increasing and spreading rapidly. Within just a few months this health conscious and physically fit former marine dropped 30 pounds and couldn't keep food down. Doctors were at a loss as to the cause of these symptoms. Eventually, doctors at John Hopkins hospital diagnosed Stephen with diffuse scleroderma, an extremely rare disease with no cure and in his case fatal.

Subsequently, Stephen poured himself into the writing of this book working tirelessly through increasing pain, hardening of joints and inner organs, bouts of hospitalizations and eventually passing away in 2014. He never complained, and pushed himself to complete this book perhaps sensing time might be limited.

This book is the result of Stephen's research on the topic of tithing and his desire to offer an approach to tithing based on Scripture. It was Stephen's fervent hope that this book would help believers adopt a balanced approach to tithing allowing the WWCOG and its members to prosper both financially and spiritually.

1

THE MENTION OF MONEY

There are many references to money in both the old and new covenants, but there are no references to, nor specific examples of, tithing money anywhere in the Bible. Some people erroneously believe that Israel tithed crops and certain animals because money was not commonly used at that time. The Bible reveals that money was used by Israel before entering the land of Canaan, and money was used by various nations well over six hundred years before God gave Israel His laws on tithing.

Money is first mentioned in the Bible in Genesis 17:12 relating to the covenant that God made with Abraham. Genesis 17:13 says, "He who is born in your house and he who is bought with money must be circumcised." In Genesis 37:28, Joseph's brothers sold him to Midianite traders for twenty shekels of silver. In Genesis 42:2–5 Jacob sent his sons to buy grain with money in Egypt where Joseph was second in command at that time. In Genesis 23:13–20, after years of nomadic wandering, Abraham purchased for "four hundred shekels of silver the currency of the merchants" a small piece of land for a burial place in Canaan, which was promised to his descendants. Genesis 33:19 states that Jacob bought land "for one hundred pieces of money." During the time of the judges, before Israel had human kings, Delilah betrayed Samson, enticing him to discover the source of his great strength for money. The money came from the lords of the

Philistines, which involved every one of them giving "eleven hundred pieces of silver" (Judg. 16:5–18).

Exodus 30:13–15 reveals that the nation of Israel gave monetary offerings but that tithes only consisted of crops and specific farm animals according to the Law of Moses. Leviticus 27:1–34 gives the legislation for dedicating persons, animals, houses, and land vowed as a gift for the service of God. A monetary value or appraisal was placed on people and things that were dedicated to the Lord. Payments of money could be made for the people dedicated to the Lord. The value of the person was based on gender and age. To buy back or redeem unclean animals or a house, the priest would put a value on them, and the person buying back the items with money would add one-fifth to the appraisal.

The Bible talks about money being brought to the temple, as in 2 Chronicles 24:5–12, 34:9–17; 1 Chronicles 29:1–9; and 2 Kings 12:4–15. This money is assessment money from offerings or other freely given offerings and temple taxes. This money was used for the repair or service of the physical temple. The tithe that God commanded Israel to pay under the law never consisted of money. The purpose of the tithe was not for the maintenance or service of the temple, which is why Israel had monetary temple taxes and offerings separate from the agrarian tithe (Exod. 30:13–16, Matt. 17:24). The temple taxes and monetary offerings were used to hire masons, carpenters, construction workers, and metal workers who made articles for the house of the Lord. This money was not used to pay or hire preachers.

Some of the currency mentioned in the Bible that was used by Israel consisted of shekels of silver, darics (gold coins), talents (large round coins of iron or bronze), bekahs (half a shekel), and gerahs (small coins). Since the use of money was so common among the nations even before the time of Abraham, there are few references to bartering or trading without money in the Bible. It has been declared by some biblical scholars that there are more references to money in the Bible than any other subject.

Leviticus 27:30 states that the tithe was to come from "the seed of the land or of the fruit of the tree, is the Lord's." The seed did not produce minerals such as gold, silver, or copper. The seed did not produce gems such as emeralds, diamonds, and rubies. Ores excavated from the land were not tithed under the law that God gave Moses to give to Israel. The land that Israel was to possess was described in Deuteronomy 8:9 as "a land whose stones are iron and out of whose hills you can dig copper." The Hebrew word is the same for both copper and bronze. The specification of the fruit of the trees was a distinction from the whole tree. Wood or timber was not an item that was tithed, but wood was given as an offering to burn on the altar, as Nehemiah 10:34 and 13:31 confirm.

During the wilderness journey before Israel crossed the Jordan to inherit the land of Canaan, they bought food and water with money from the descendants of Esau who lived in Seir (Deut. 2:6). Israel sent messengers to Sihon, the king of Heshbon, and offered money for food and water before they entered the promised land (Deut. 2:28). Exodus 16:35 explains why Israel bought food before entering the promised land. Exodus 16:35 says, "And the children of Israel ate manna forty years until they came to an inhabited land; They ate manna until they came to the border of the land of Canaan." Manna ceased two days after the Passover in the promised land, according to Joshua 5:11–12.

The tithes that were required under the old covenant from the land were agrarian or predial, which means they came from the produce of the land. Under the Law of Moses, the required tithes were only consumable products or food. Fruits from the trees, crops from the field, and specific farm animals were tithed, according to Leviticus 27:30–32 and Deuteronomy 14:22. Leviticus 27:31 states that Israel could buy back or redeem agrarian tithes with money but had to add one-fifth to the value of the crops. The buying back of tithes with money confirms that tithes did not consist of money. It would be incongruous to buy back money by paying more money.

In Leviticus 27:32, concerning the tithe of the herd or the flock, it was the tenth animal that was set apart. The tenth cow or sheep or goat did not have to be without blemish or defect but only had to be the tenth one that passed under the rod. One difference between

3

the tithing of animals and the offering of animals is that animal sacrifices had to be without blemish or defect, according to Leviticus 1:10, Deuteronomy 17:1, and Leviticus 22:20–22. The tithe of the herd or flock only had to be the tenth one that passed under the rod or counted regardless of defect or not. The tithe of the herd and flock could not be bought back with money, but the tithe of crops was redeemable (Lev. 27:33). The difference between dedicated offerings and devoted offerings is that devoted offerings were irrevocable. Devoted offerings were exclusively for the Lord. Leviticus 5:14 and 2 Kings 12:15–16 confirm that money could be given for a trespass offering of a ram from the flock, but the tithe of the herd or flock were treated like devoted items, which were also not redeemable (Lev. 27:28).

God was specific as to what was His concerning tithes. If a man only had nine sheep, he was not required to tithe on small amounts consisting of less than ten. If a man had nineteen sheep, only one was tithed to God—even though one out of nineteen is not 10 percent. It was not the first one counted that belonged to God but the tenth one that God claimed to "be holy to the Lord" (Lev. 27:32). Tithes of animals consisted of the herd and flock, so only particular farm animals were tithed. There was no tithing of unclean animals such as swine, camels, and donkeys. There was no tithing of wild animals such as deer, quails, and fish, according to the Law of Moses.

Deuteronomy 14:25 states that the (festival) tithe of crops and livestock could be exchanged for money *if* the journey to the feast was too long, so that they were not able to carry all the crops. This also confirms that tithes under the old covenant did not involve money but could be exchanged for money under certain conditions. Deuteronomy 14:26 reveals that the money, which came from the exchange of tithes, was to be spent for feasting or eating a sacrificial meal before the Lord.

A feast of thanksgiving occurred for seven days for God's blessing on the harvest. The eighth day was a separate holy day connected to the feast (Lev. 23:36). The holy days in Leviticus 23 are referred to as feasts, and the harvest festivals included celebratory meals that required gathering in the fruit of the land (Lev. 23:39). Money could be exchanged under certain conditions for the agrarian tithes in order to celebrate these physical feasts of the physical harvest.

Interestingly, the Pilgrims instituted the feast of thanksgiving, which was originally a religious feast in November based on the old covenant ordinance of the feast of ingathering. The Bible records how Israel gathered in the crops of the land and brought a tithe of the produce to Jerusalem to celebrate the fall harvest (Lev. 23:39, Deut. 14:22). Under the new covenant we serve God in the newness of the Spirit, which offers a spiritual harvest that we need to be aware of so that we can celebrate our fabulous future.

Under the old covenant, a man would pay "fifty shekels of silver" to the father of his bride if he lies with her, and they are found out (Deut. 22:29). Fines of one hundred shekels of silver were paid for deceitfully detesting virgins, according to the miscellaneous and sexual morality laws of the old covenant (Deut. 22:17–19). Restitution money was paid for acts of violence that caused injury (Exod. 21:19). Exodus 21:32–36 mentions monetary fines enforced under the law. Exodus 22:4–7 mentions fines for stolen goods and for damaged property. Israel was not to charge interest on money to a fellow Israelite but could charge interest on money or food to a foreigner (Deut. 23:20). Charging interest, or usury, was a practice among many Gentile nations and originated from Babylon, which goes back to Nimrod in Genesis 10.

Wages were paid to occupations such as soldiers (2 Sam. 10:6); shepherds (John 12–13); fishermen (Mark 1:10); masons and carpenters (2 Chron. 24:12); stonecutters and construction workers (2 Kings 12:11–12); farm laborers (Matt. 20:1–16); prostitutes (Deut. 23:18); nurses (Exod. 2:9); perfumers, cooks, bakers (1 Sam. 8:13); potters, leather workers, metal workers, and silversmiths (Acts 19:24); clothe makers, beer and wine brewers, lumber workers, sandal makers, tanners, weaving or workers of fabrics (1 Chron. 4:21); tax collectors, gem cutters, jewelry makers, and miners. These are a few of the many occupations among ancient Israel that brought in a monetary income. Acts 19:19 reveals that authors who sold books especially on magic were very successful during the time of Paul the apostle, and this is still common today. In both the old and new covenant, soothsaying or fortune-telling was a lucrative business (Acts 16:16).

God gave bylaws for the Israelite farmers who inherited land to tithe crops and specific farm animals. Nowhere in the Bible are there instructions for the wage earners of various professions or occupations to tithe money from their wages. Deuteronomy 24:14–15 talks about hired servants or wage earners who were poor should not be oppressed and were to be paid daily. In Malachi 3:5, God's judgment includes being a swift witness against sorcerers, adulterers, perjurers, and those who exploit wage earners. Wage earners were generally paid money daily for their labor during the time that the Bible was written (Deut. 24:14–15). Exploit means to make use of selfishly, unethically, or to take advantage of others. Exploitation is also addressed in the new covenant as a practice of corrupt teachers.

Any church governance that enforces a monetary tax or tithe on what members earn to pay preachers is exploitation, since the Word does not endorse this. Second Peter 2:1–3 talks about false teachers among God's people who "by covetousness will exploit you with deceptive words." Some translations say, "with feigned words make merchandise of you." Among God's church it says, "MANY will follow their destructive ways" (2 Pet. 2:2).

Many teachers are involved in following the destructive heresies that have been brought in among the brethren. The exploitation among the churches today is massive, and many are involved in this iniquity. When the Bible says "many" this implies the majority. Second Peter 2:13–16 reveals how this exploitation relates to "following the way of Balaam, who loved the wages of unrighteousness." Following the way of Balaam involves loving the pay that they acquire deceitfully.

When it comes to eschatology, there is much written in the old covenant that pertains to us living in this end-time. We are repeatedly warned about the destruction brought about by corrupt shepherds, or pastors, and false prophets among God's people. The new covenant writings expound on the things written by the prophets that are relevant for us today. The history of physical Israel is being repeated in many ways through the new covenant church. Nehemiah 9:30 states: "Yet for many years You had patience with them, And testified against them by Your Spirit in Your prophets. Yet they would not listen."

The true prophets of God had much to say about the false prophets among them. Jesus the prophet like Moses (Deut. 18:15) also warned us about the deceit of false prophets. Matthew 24:11–12 says, "Then many false prophets will rise up and deceive many. And because lawlessness will abound, the love of many will grow cold." Paul was persuaded that nothing can separate us from the love of God or God's love for us (Rom. 8:38–39). Romans 5:8 says, "But God demonstrates His own love toward us, in that while we were still sinners, Christ died for us." The abounding of iniquity can cause the agape love that we have to depart or wax cold from us. This prophecy in Matthew 24 is being fulfilled within the churches of God today.

Jeremiah, like many of the prophets, warns us about deceitful prophets. Jeremiah even reveals how God can use false prophets to lead others to conversion. Jeremiah 23:22 says, "But if they (profane prophets) had stood in My counsel, And had caused My people to hear My words, then they would have turned them from their evil way and from the evil of their doings." The words of God can be spoken by false or corrupt prophets, and Balaam is an example of this. It is not the prophet who converts; the Word converts. Profane preachers may even teach the truth on just about everything else except tithing because the false teaching on tithing is one of the ways that they covet, control, exploit, deceive, and destroy.

Numbers 18:19–28 explains how the Levites were entitled to the tithes of crops and animals as an inheritance in return for their service of the physical temple. Numbers 18:26–28 reveals that a tenth of the tithe went to the Aaronic priesthood. All the sons of Aaron were Levites, but not all Levites were descendants of Aaron. The Levites were the one tribe that did not inherit farming land, so the Levites had a command from God to take agrarian tithes from the promised land as an inheritance according to the law (Num. 18:26, Heb. 7:5).

Numbers 18:24–26 confirms that tithes came from the children of Israel and not from Gentiles or strangers who were hired servants among Israel. Numbers 18:24 says, "For the tithes of (from) the children of Israel which they offer up as a heave offering to the Lord, I (God) have given to the Levites as an inheritance, therefore I have said to them, among the children of Israel they shall have no inheritance." One thing that the Levites, widows, orphans, and strangers who were often wage earners among Israel all had in common is that they were not recipients of the inheritance of land that God gave Israel. God made provisions from the tithes of the land for those among Israel who were not owners of farming land (Deut. 14:27–29). Malachi 3:8 says, "Bring all the tithes into the storehouse." This is talking about a tithe of the tithe. One percent of the tithe went to the storehouse at the physical temple where dried fruit and grains were stored. It was the Levites' responsibility to bring this 1 percent—a tithe of the tithe—to the storehouse. Nehemiah 10:38 states: "And the Priest, the descendants of Aaron, shall be with the Levites when the Levites shall bring up a tenth of the tithe to the house of our God, to the rooms of the storehouse." Tithes were delivered to the forty-eight cities of the Levites (Num. 35:3–8). The Levites brought a tithe of the tithe to the temple for the Aaronic priesthood, according to Numbers 18:26–28.

Nehemiah 12:44 says, "And at the same time some were appointed over the rooms of the storehouse for the offerings, the first fruits, and the tithes, to gather into them from the fields of the cities the portions specified by the law for the priest and Levites." Nehemiah 10:37–39 reiterates that tithes for the priests went to the storerooms at the temple storehouse. These tithes came from the Levites who received tithes from the farming of the Israelite landowners.

Nehemiah 10:35–39 talks about ordinances to bring fruit from the ground and from the trees and tithes from the land "to the storerooms of the house of our God; and to bring the tithes of our land to the Levites, for the Levites should receive the tithes in all our farming communities." People could make monetary profits from hunting and fishing and selling all kinds of merchandise and doing various types of labor, but the tithes under the law only came from certain farm animals and the edible produce of the land of their inheritance.

The tithes consisting of crops and specific farm animals were holy to the Lord (Lev. 27:30–32). Nehemiah 12:47 mentions how Israel consecrated or set apart holy things for the Levites, and the Levites consecrated them for the children of Aaron. Leviticus 27:9 states that offerings and "all that anyone gives to the Lord shall be holy." When we truly give our lives to God then we also shall be holy. First Peter 1:16 says, "because it is written, Be holy for I am holy."

Difference between Storehouse and Treasury

The storehouse was a separate part of the temple where food—a tithe of the tithe of crops—was stored. Malachi 3:10 says, "Bring all the tithes into the storehouse, that there may be FOOD in my house." The treasury was in the temple court of the woman where people gave monetary offerings instead of tithes. Luke 21:1–4 and Mark 12:41–44 talk about the poor widow who gave an offering of two mites into the treasury. This poor widow had the right to receive food from the tithe specified in the law, but her choice to give an offering was voluntary. The widow contributed two mites, and in the Greek language a mite was a lepta, which was a small copper coin. Mark 12:42 reveals that two mites were equivalent to a farthing or quadrans, which were Roman coins.

Commerce at the temple involved those who bought and sold doves and animals for sacrificing, which took place in the court of the Gentiles (Matt. 21:12). While Jesus was on earth there are numerous references to the marketplaces, which were set up along some of the main streets or in the town square. A farmer could pay a tithe of his crops to the Levites and still make a profit on the other 90 percent of his crops, which generally would have been way more than what even the largest of the families would have consumed. In Luke 17:28 Jesus said that even in the time of Lot the people bought and sold. Marketing and the use of money was an ancient and common custom. Roman coins and foreign forms of currency were deemed unacceptable for temple offerings, which is why they had money changers at the temple who were making excessive profits on their transactions. Matthew 21:12 says, "Then Jesus went into the temple of God and drove out all those who bought and sold in the temple and over-turned the tables of the money changers and the seats of those who sold doves." Men have cunningly devised ways to make God's house a "den of thieves" and religion a business for manipulating money. Not all money was accepted at the temple for offerings. Deuteronomy 23:18 states: "you shall not bring the wages of a harlot or the price of a dog (male prostitute) to the house of the Lord your God for any vowed offering, for both of these are an abomination to the Lord your God." In Matthew 27:5 when Judas threw his thirty pieces of silver in the temple, it was not accepted in the treasury. Matthew 27:26 says, "but the chief priest took the silver pieces and said, "it is not lawful to put them into the treasury, because they are the price of blood." The Bible talks about monetary offerings, and the law of Moses included a monetary temple tax (Matt. 17:24). Exodus 30:13 says, "This is what everyone among those who are numbered shall give: half a shekel according to the shekel of the sanctuary (a shekel is twenty gerahs). The half-shekel shall be an offering to the Lord." Offerings also included the giving of money, but there are no ordinances for tithing money anywhere in the Bible.

2

THE THREE PURPOSES FOR TITHES

When we comprehend the intent of the tithe it should be evident as to why tithes were not monetary. Understanding the reason for tithes also explains why tithing is not applicable to the new covenant. The Bible reveals three purposes for tithes. The first reason for tithes of the agricultural products was for an inheritance for the Levites. The Levites did not inherit farming land since they were set apart solely for the service of the physical temple. This tithe was also known as the Levitical tithe or a heave offering (Num. 18:24–28). Heave offerings did not consist of money but were only agricultural products. The old covenant tithe was an emolument for the office of the Levites.

The second use for the agricultural tithe was to take to Jerusalem for a sacrificial meal of thanksgiving (Deut. 14:22–23). These physical feasts of thanksgiving were acknowledgments of God's blessings on the land and the covenant with physical Israel. Deuteronomy 8:10 says, "When you have eaten and are full, then you shall bless (give thanks to) the Lord your God for the good land which He has given you." Israel was to rejoice over the abundance that God gave as a result of their obedience under the law (Deut. 28:1–14). The blessings of God reflected Israel's rapprochement with God, which was something to celebrate. The third use for the agricultural tithes every third year of the sabbatical cycle was to feed the poor nonlandowners. The Bible does not specify that the third year of tithing was an additional tithe or a third tithe. The nebulous distinction in the law of the number of tithes make it a polemical issue. The fact that these ordinances are not pertinent to the new covenant is clearly validated by the Word. The terms first, second, or third tithe are nonbiblical terms.

Deuteronomy 14:28 explains that every third year, not every third "tithe" year, the tithe of the produce consisting of fruits and grains was to be stored locally "within your gates." Deuteronomy 14:29 explains that this tithe was given to the Levites because they have "no portion nor inheritance" with the other tribes, also the strangers, fatherless and widows so that they could eat. Deuteronomy 26:12 also talks about how God gave in the third year the tithe to the Levites, strangers, fatherless, and widows, "so that they may eat within your gates and be filled."

One of the reasons for tithing crops or food was so that everyone could eat the fruit of the land. The third year of tithing was not just given to the Levites but was shared with all the nonlandowners among Israel, which included the Levites, widows, fatherless, and strangers. The strangers were the foreigners who dwelt among Israel. Under the law of Moses, tithes were always food—consumable products—which is why words such as *food*, *eat*, and *feasting* are associated with tithing (Deut. 12:17–18, 14:23, 14:26, 26:14; Num. 18:11; Mal. 3:10). The third year of sharing tithes plus allowing the poor to glean the fields were some of the ways God showed fairness to the poor. Deuteronomy 10:18 says, "He (God) administers justice for the fatherless and the widow and loves the stranger, giving him food and clothing."

When it came to gleaning after the reapers in Deuteronomy 24:19–21, the Levites were not included with the widows, strangers, and fatherless because the Levites were provided with a tithe of crops so they would not have to work in the fields. The Levites were given totally to the service of the temple, and gleaning fields was a hard job that would have interfered with their work of the temple. The Bible does not teach that the purpose for tithes was for the funding of preaching the gospel or for paying hirelings or pastors.

First Timothy 5:3–4 talks about supporting widows who are really widows. Paul's instructions are for the children or grandchildren to take care of the widow first, but if a widow is alone without family and conducts herself in a godly way, then the church should support her. There is no mention of tithes to support widows under the new covenant. Contributions freely given and alms were originally the means for helping the needy under the new covenant.

Under the old covenant the inheritance was passed down from fathers to sons (Num. 36). Under the old covenant, if a man had only daughters, then they had to marry within their tribe so that the inheritance would remain within the tribe of the fathers. The inheritance was then passed down from the father to the son-in-law through the daughter. The inheritance was not passed down from mothers or widows.

Under the law of Moses, the firstborn son would receive a double portion of all that the father has. This inheritance law is mentioned in Deuteronomy 21:17. The widow or wife did not receive an inheritance under the old covenant, so provisions were made to take care of widows through the agrarian tithes. Colossians 1:15 refers to Jesus as "He is the image of the invisible God, the firstborn over all creation." The pinnacle of God's creation is His own family with Jesus being the firstborn.

Colossians 1:18 refers to Jesus as "the firstborn from the dead that in all things He may have preeminence." Without the resurrection of Christ there would be no eternal life for mankind. Birth is designed where the head of the body is to come out first. All who have the indwelling of the Holy Spirit are the children of God (1 John 3:2, Gal. 4:6). Jesus is referred to as "the only begotten of the Father" (John 3:16 and 1:14) since no one else has been resurrected to the glory of God at this time (Col. 3:4, 1 Cor. 15:51–55, 1 Thess. 4:14–16, Rom. 1:4).

The old covenant had the leviratic law stating that if a man died without children, the brother or close relative would perform the duty of a husband to perpetuate the name of the dead through his inheritance (Deut. 25:5–10). Boaz marrying Ruth was an example of the leviratic law since Boaz was a close relative of Ruth's deceased husband (Ruth 4:5–10). Boaz fulfilled the role of kinsman-redeemer. Ruth and Boaz end up being the great-grandparents of king David and part of the lineage of Jesus. Ruth was a Moabite who chose the God of Israel to be her God (Ruth 1:16). The book of Ruth portrays the marriage after the end of the harvest of the first fruits, or Pentecost (Ruth 2:23, 4:10). Revelation 19:7–9 addresses the marriage of the Lamb with the first fruits to God.

Celebrating the Old and New Covenant Harvests

Under the old covenant, the Israelites tithed crops to take to Jerusalem where the temple was, which was where God placed His name. The agrarian tithe was established for a physical feast, which was a celebration of the physical harvest, which was a part of the physical inheritance that God gave to physical Israel. Under the new covenant, it is not a physical feast that is preeminent, but God wants us to feast spiritually on His word (John 6:58, 6:63). The words of Jesus are the words of eternal life (John 6:68). Romans 14:17 says, "for the kingdom of God is not eating and drinking, but righteousness and peace and joy in the Holy Spirit."

The harvest we celebrate under the new covenant was revealed by Jesus in parables. Matthew 13:24–50 is a parable is about a resurrection that separates the wheat from the tares. Matthew 13:29–30 says, "Let both grow together until the harvest, and at the time of harvest I will say to the reapers, "First gather together the tares and bind them in bundles to burn them, but gather the wheat into my barn." Among God's church we have the wheat from God and the tares from the enemy growing together. Matthew 13:39 says, "the harvest is the end of the age." At the end of this age the saints—being the wheat among the tares—shall be harvested into God's barn, symbolic of the kingdom of God.

Revelation 14:15–16 also mentions the spiritual harvest of our resurrection into the kingdom of God. The harvest of people is also mentioned in Matthew 9:37–38, which says, "The harvest truly is plentiful but the laborers are few. Therefore pray the Lord of the harvest to send out laborers into His harvest." The bringing in of the soon coming spiritual harvest of God involves a work in which all the servants of God should participate.

The feast of tabernacles was also called the feast of ingathering (Exod. 34:22, Lev. 23:39). After gathering crops from the harvest, a tithe of the harvest was used to celebrate the harvest (Deut. 14:22–23). This old covenant feast also depicts when saints will be gathered into the kingdom (Matt. 13:47–48, 24:31). The symbolic meanings of the physical ordinances of the old covenant are revealed to the chosen and elect (Luke 8:10).

Physical Israel celebrated their corruptible inheritance of a fertile land. Under the new covenant, the saints are to celebrate the impending incorruptible inheritance of the kingdom of God. First Peter 1:4 says, "to an inheritance incorruptible and undefiled and that does not fade away, reserved in heaven for you." Hebrews 9:15 says, "Those who are called may receive the promise of the eternal inheritance."

Deuteronomy chapters 27 and 28 expound on the blessings for obedience and the curses for disobedience under the old covenant. The blessings under the old covenant for physical Israel were physical and mainly related to the land of their inheritance. Under the new covenant the blessings are primarily spiritual. Ephesians 1:3 says, "Blessed be the God and Father of our Lord Jesus Christ, who has blessed us with every spiritual blessing in heavenly places in Christ." Jesus emphasized the importance of realizing how blessed we are in Matthew 5:3–14, which is also called the beatitudes.

Physical blessings are not excluded under the new covenant, but they are secondary. Third John 2 says, "Beloved, I pray that you prosper in all things and be in health, just as your soul prospers." The main thing that we need to do is mentioned in Matthew 6:33, which says, "But seek first the kingdom of God and His righteousness and all these things shall be added to you." What God wants us to seek first is the spiritual. The physical things that we see are secondary. Second Corinthians 4:18 says, "while we do not look at the things which are seen, but at the things which are not seen. For the things which are seen are temporary, but the things which are not seen are eternal." It takes faith to look at the things that are not seen.

Before Israel inherited the promised land, there were no tithing requirements given to Israel. Tithing was a part of the law of Moses that was added because of sin (Gal. 3:19). Deuteronomy 12:1, 10–11 mention statutes and judgments for Israel to carefully observe in the land (not in the wilderness) that they were about to inherit. These judgments and statutes included specific instructions for tithing crops after they inherited the land and reaped the harvest. This tithe was an annual event that occurred "year by year" (Deut. 14:22).

Israel came out of Egypt with articles of silver, gold, clothing, great spoils, and herds and flocks, and even "a great deal of livestock" (Exod. 12:32–38, Psalm 105:37). There were no requirements to tithe while they wandered in the wilderness looking to inherit the promised land. The church today is in a spiritual wilderness on a journey to receive an inheritance, which is the kingdom of God. Before Israel could receive their inheritance they had to be humble and be tested to see whether they would keep God's commandments or not, according to Deuteronomy 8:2. It is important that we learn from what is written or recorded in God's word so that we do not make the same mistakes that Israel made.

The Ten Commandments were "the way" God commanded (Deut. 9:12, 9:16). The Ten Commandments are the way of the Way, which is Jesus (John 14:6). Jesus said in Matthew 7:14: "Because narrow is the gate and difficult is the way which leads to life, and there are few who find it." It can be difficult to not fit in with the majority, but God called us to be the few, the humble, the minority. Christianity is also referred to as "the Way" in the book of Acts. The servants of God "proclaimed the way of salvation" as mentioned in Acts 16:17.

In Acts 24:14 Paul said, "But this I confess to you, that according to the Way which they call a sect, so I worship the God of my fathers, believing all things which are written in the Law and in the Prophets." Paul knew and believed that the tithes under the law consisted of agrarian products. Paul also knew that the tithes for the

Levites were not something that he had the right to claim for himself since he was of the tribe of Benjamin. As an apostle, Paul understood that he could accept offerings, but for the most part he chose not to use this right, according to 1 Corinthians 9:12–19.

A covenant is an agreement. The law, or Pentateuch, is comprised of various covenants. Besides the covenant with Israel, covenants were made with people such as Noah, Abraham, Phinehas, and David. The covenant with Levi pertaining to the priesthood was an additional covenant within the law mentioned in Numbers 25:12–13. The tablets of stone that God wrote on were "the words of the covenant, the Ten Commandments," according to Exodus 34:28.

The Ten Commandments involved an agreement where God would show "mercy to thousands, to those who love Him and keep His commandments" (Exod. 20:6). God's covenant of mercy has not been done away with under the new covenant. It is through God's mercy that we can be saved. Jude 21 says, "keep yourselves in the love of our Lord Jesus Christ, looking for the mercy of our Lord Jesus Christ unto eternal life." Titus 3:5 says, "not by works of righteousness which we have done, but according to His mercy He saved us."

When we fail to keep the perfect law perfectly, we can still obtain mercy because of God's forgiveness, kindness, and grace. First John 1:9 says, "If we confess our sins, He is faithful and just to forgive us our sins and to cleanse us from all unrighteousness." Christ loved the church to sanctify and cleanse us "with the washing of water by the word (Eph. 5:26). Titus 3:5 also says, "He saved us, through the washing of regeneration and renewing of the Holy Spirit." Our being renewed after the image of Christ is accomplished by the Holy Spirit (living water) through the Word.

A mixed multitude left Egypt along with the Israelites. The mixed multitude could have included various races besides the Egyptians. Interracial marriage was also prevalent among Israel (Deut. 21:11). Even the genealogy of Jesus involved various women of non-Israelite descent (Luke 3:23–38, Matt. 1:1–17). The non-Israelites of the exodus included servants bought with money and hired servants, according to Exodus 12:44–45.The non-Israelites were not included as recipients of the inheritance of the land promised to Abraham and his descendants (Gen. 12:7). Since the Israelites used money even before they crossed over into the promised land, the plundering of the Egyptians in Exodus 12:36 apparently included money.

Biblical Sharecropping

Tithing was biblical sharecropping. Tennant farmers paid a share (a tithe) of the crops as a type of rent or tax levied from the land. Tenant is defined as one who pays rent to use or occupy property owned by another. In Leviticus 25:23 God says, "the land shall not be sold permanently, for the land is mine; for you are strangers and sojourners with me." The Israelites were tenants on the land, and ownership was temporary since the physical earth and heaven will pass away.

Matthew 24:35 says, "Heaven and earth will pass away, but My words will by no means pass away." Hebrews 1:10–11 also talk about the physical heavens and earth perishing. Second Peter 3:13 mentions the coming of the "new heavens and a new earth in which righteousness dwells." Revelation 21:1 also mentions the new heaven and earth, "for the first heaven and the first earth had passed away." The inheritance of the meek under the new covenant will include the new earth (Matt. 5:5). Joel 3:1–2 prophesized that in the end-time, God will gather all nations at Armageddon and bring them down to the valley of Jehoshaphat. God still refers to this land as His land, which He claimed for His heritage Israel. Ezekiel 40 through 48, Amos 9:15, and other scriptures relate to the millennium reign of Christ and how Israel will return to the land that God gave to them. The Bible reiterates that all the earth is the Lord's (Exod. 19:5, Ps. 24:1, 1 Cor. 10:26).

Paying tithes of crops to Levites acknowledged God's ownership of the land and that the Levites belonged to God in place of the firstborn (Num. 3:12–13). What was owed to God, the Supreme landowner, was given to the Levites by God as an inheritance. Numbers 18:20–21 says, "Then the Lord said to Aaron; 'You shall have no inheritance in their land, nor shall you have any portion among them; I am your portion and your inheritance among the children of Israel. Behold, I have given the children of Levi all the tithes in Israel as an inheritance in return for the work which they perform, the work of the tabernacle of meeting.'"

No one besides the Levites have the right to take for themselves what God specified as being an inheritance for the Levites. The old covenant inheritance was physical and temporary, but the new covenant inheritance is spiritual and eternal. The sharing of crops or tithes with the poor nonlandowners reflects how important it is to God to help the needy. Blessings are bestowed on all people who comply with God's way (Deut. 16:14, 10:18).

Sharecropping also occurred in Egypt when Joseph was second in command under Pharaoh. In Genesis 47:13–26 during the time of famine, Joseph gathered up all the money found in Egypt and Canaan for grain which the people bought (Gen. 47:14). When the money was all spent, then people exchanged livestock for bread. Eventually people sold their land and themselves to Pharaoh in exchange for food. When the famine was over, the people became sharecroppers (Gen. 47:24–26). Two-tenths or one-fifth of the harvest was paid to Pharaoh, the proprietor. The rest of the crops were for the servants and their families. The priests of Egypt were exempt from sharecropping since they did not have to sell their land because rations were allotted to them by Pharaoh (Gen. 47:22).

Leviticus 25 mentions how every seventh year there is to be a rest or Sabbath for the land. Every seventh year Israel was not required to tithe from the land, and nothing was sown or reaped. Whatever the land produced in the sabbatical year was free for anyone to eat. Leviticus 25:21 states that God provided enough produce the sixth year to last for three years, so farmers would not be lacking in the seventh year. The seventh year was a rest from the crops levied or tithed from the land.

Agrarianism and Feudalism

One reason why Israel tithed crops instead of money is because of agrarianism, which was the movement for impartial distribution of land applied among the tribes of Israel. The exclusion of the Levites from the inheritance of land was compensated by the other tribes paying agrarian tithes. One of the reasons for the numbering of the people in the book of Numbers was so that the larger tribes in number would receive larger portions of land. The Levites were not included in the numbering of the people (Num. 1:47). Since the Levites did not inherit farming land, they inherited the tithes from the land (Num. 18:24).

The agrarian tithes from the land acknowledged the vassalage of Israel for God's blessing on the land. The agrarian tithes were required because of the feudalism of the old covenant. Feudalism involved a landowner granting land to a vassal, subordinate, or dependent in return for service and allegiance. Disobedience to God took away God's blessings, which also included protection from the enemy.

When Judah's kings did evil in the sight of the Lord, they were eventually overrun by enemies. Second Kings 23:33 mentions that the Pharaoh of Egypt put Jehoahaz in prison and imposed on the land a tribute. In 2 Kings 23:35 Jehoiakim, king of Judah, was commanded by Pharaoh to have the people pay taxes to Egypt. In 2 Kings 24:1 when Babylon defeated the Egyptians, Jehoiakim became a vassal to Nebuchadnezzar, king of Babylon.

The promised land was to be evidence of God's blessings as the superlative landlord. Some of the ways that Israel was to serve God in the land was by the sharing of crops with the poor among them and by paying a tithe of the crops to the Levites. The Levites belonged to God and were set apart for the service of the earthly temple. Numbers 3:45 and Numbers 3:12–13 affirm that God claimed the Levites for Himself. The promised land mentioned in Deuteronomy 19:8 is also called the holy land in Zechariah 2:12. This land was to be used for the service of God and for God's service to man.

Deuteronomy 11:12 says that the promised land was "a land for which the Lord your God cares; the eyes of the Lord your God are always on it, from the beginning of the year to the very end of the year." God reiterates that the land Israel inherited belonged to Him, and even the nation of Israel belonged to God. Psalm 135:4 says,

"For the Lord has chosen Jacob for Himself, Israel for His special treasure," or precious possession. God claimed Israel as His wife (Jer. 3:14, Isa. 54:5). A husband should view his wife as a special treasure.

Israel was to be the sheep of God's pasture (Ps. 79:13, 95:7, Ezek. 34:31). The pasture was a place for food (Ezek. 34:14). God is the one who provides the physical and spiritual food needed for life. Jesus said in John 10:9: "I am the door. If anyone enters by Me, he will be saved, and will go in and out and find pasture." Matthew 16:19 mentions "the keys of the kingdom." The word *keys* is plural. These keys include both the Word and the Spirit, which are intrinsic for entering the door of life. Israel was purchased by God, and Israel was His inheritance by being the sheep of His pasture (Ps. 74:1–2, 28:9, Deut. 9:29).

The pagan nations prayed to their pagan gods of fertility to make their land, wives, and livestock fertile. When Israel turned away from God's way in the wilderness, they made a molded calf (Exod. 32:1–8). This golden calf was a replica of the Egyptian god Apis. The Egyptians worshiped this idol, which they believed would bring them prosperity. Israel was meant to be a witness that their God was the One who gives the increase of the seed in their wives, animals, and land. Deuteronomy 7:13 states: "He (God) will also bless the fruit of your womb and the fruit of your land, your grain and your new wine and your oil, the increase of your cattle and the offspring of your flock, in the land of which He swore to your fathers to give you." A land of milk and honey (the consumable gold) symbolized fertility and prosperity from God.

The Tithing of Abraham

Tithing is first mentioned in the Bible in Genesis 14:20 when Abraham freely gave a tithe of the spoils to Melchizedek out of his own volition. The Bible states that Abraham gave a tithe of the spoils, but false prophets may change a word and say that Abraham paid tithes to Melchizedek which is incorrect. Paying and giving are two totally different things. The Bible does not say Abraham paid tithes, which would have meant that it was mandatory. Apparently, the men who were with Abram did not tithe from their portion of the spoils and were without reproach (Gen. 14:24).

Abraham did not tithe according to the law of Moses since the laws for tithing were not established at that time. Under the law of Moses, the tithing of spoils was never required. The law of Moses involved matters pertaining to the Levitical priesthood that did not exist during the time of Abraham. The law of Moses came around 430 years after Israel's sojourn in Egypt (Exod. 12:40). The law of Moses came about 645 years after the initial promise of land was given to Abraham.

The law also included the Ten Commandments, which is a deontological decree for all generations (Deut. 7:9). First John 5:2–3 says, "By this we know that we love the children of God when we love God and keep His commandments. For this is the love of God, that we keep His commandments. And His commandments are not burdensome." It is the commandments of men that are not according to the Word, such as monetary tithing, that can be burdensome. The Ten Commandments declare the way to have a right relationship with God and our neighbor.

There are various examples of Israel taking spoils from other nations and in some cases a small offering or tribute of about 1 or 2 percent was offered from the spoils (Num. 31:25–41). Even before Israel crossed the Jordan, they took spoils for themselves from the Egyptians and Amorites, but there were no commands for Israel to tithe spoils under the law. Some examples of Israel taking spoils without paying tithes include Numbers 31:25–41; Deuteronomy 2:35, 3:7, 20:14; 1 Chronicles 26:27; 2 Chronicles 15:11; and Exodus 12:35–36. Under the Mosaic law, it was evident that the tithing of spoils was not practiced. Tithing was a common custom throughout the ancient Near East and Mesopotamia area where Abraham was from. The Egyptians, Babylonians, Persians, and almost all Gentile nations had a tithing system incorporated in their government. Tithing was an ancient heathen taxing policy and ecumenical custom. Tithing was not something neoteric even during the time of Abraham. The book of Maccabees records that the Seleucid kings of Syria and other

Gentile nations viewed tithes as a source of royal income. Monetary tithing became a nonbiblical ecclesiastical custom instituted by men under the new covenant.

Abraham chose to give a tithe of the spoils as a gift to Melchizedek, which also was an acknowledgment of Melchizedek's kingship. To present a king with a gift and even a tithe from battle was a common custom in ancient times. Presenting a tithe of spoils was also an acknowledgment of the fact that Melchizedek was the priest anointed by God who proclaimed the victory in battle. Genesis 14 reveals how Abram was the one being blessed by God. Genesis 14:19–20 says, "And blessed be Abram of God Most High, Possessor of heaven and earth; And blessed be God Most High, who has delivered your enemies into your hand."

Some try to use this onetime example of Abraham freely giving a tithe of spoils, which was not a requirement under the old covenant, as a basis for commanding tithing under the new covenant. This corroborates the fact that no new covenant scriptures support monetary tithing. The scriptures do not specify what the spoils consisted of, but we do know that the spoils involved food that was eaten by the three men who went with Abram (Gen. 14:24). Consider this, Abraham went to war, gave a burnt offering, was physically circumcised, and had a child by a concubine or second wife while being married to Sarah. Just because Abraham did certain things does not mean that we are required to do them today.

We know Jacob made a vow that was conditional to tithe. In Genesis 28:20, Jacob started the vow by saying *if*. This vow was based on receiving protection and blessings that involved receiving land. A vow is defined as a voluntary pledge to fulfill an agreement. Jacob died in Egypt and never received the promised land in his physical life, so we do not have any examples in the Bible of Jacob tithing anything. The descendants of Jacob inherited the land after the exodus from Egypt. When Israel inherited the promised land, then specific laws on what to tithe from the land were applied to Jacob's descendants under the old covenant.

Today in America we have a tax system under our government

that was derived or reformed from the ancient pagan custom of tithing. The original tax was a tithe. The church is to represent the kingdom of God, but we are still required to comply with man's government as long as it does not cause us to violate God's law (Titus 3:1, 1 Pet. 2:13, Rom. 13:1–7). We are obligated to pay taxes to man's government, which still exercises authority over us although "our citizenship is in heaven," according to Philippians 3:20.

In Matthew 22:17 when Jesus was asked, "Is it lawful to pay taxes to Caesar or not?" Jesus replied, "Show me the tax money," and He said, "Whose image and inscription is this?" They said Caesar's, and Jesus said, "Render therefore to Caesar the things that are Caesar's and to God the things that are God's." Caesar's image was stamped on the tax money, which was also why Roman coins were not accepted by the Jews for the temple offerings. Christians belong to God so when we render to God the things that are God's, we should do as Romans 12:1 says, "present your bodies a living sacrifice, holy, acceptable to God, which is your reasonable service." When it comes to presenting ourselves as a living sacrifice, I do not think that any of us want to give God just 10 percent, but all of us should endeavor to give God at least 100 percent.

God's image is stamped on His people who are called by His name and become a new creation in Christ (2 Cor. 5:17). Ephesians 4:24 says, "Put on the new man which was created according to God, in true righteousness and holiness." The work of God in Genesis 1:26 of making man in His image and likeness is still being worked out today. Ephesians 2:10 says, "For we are His workmanship created in Christ Jesus for good works, which God prepared beforehand that we should walk in them." We are a work in progress. Philippians 1:6 says, "being confident of this very thing, that He who has begun a good work in you will complete it until the day of Jesus Christ." Philippians 2:13 says, "for it is God who works in you both to will and to do for His good pleasure."

Our good works are to glorify our Father in heaven because it is God working in us through Jesus Christ (Matt. 5:16, Heb. 13:21). John 6:29 says, "This is the work of God, that you believe in Him whom He sent." The Word gives a definition of a believer. John 14:12 says, "Most assuredly, I say to you, he who believes in Me, the works that I do he will do also." Titus 3:8 says, "This is a faithful saying, and these things I want you to affirm constantly, that those who have believed in God should be careful to maintain good works. These things are good and profitable to men."

John 14:12 also says, "And greater works than these he will do, because I go to My Father." Jesus did many great works while He was on earth. He healed the sick, gave sight to the blind, fed the multitudes, turned water into wine, cast out demons, and raised the dead among many other works. The ultimate work of Christ involves salvation. Psalm 74:12 says, "For God is my King from of old, working salvation in the midst of the earth." After all the miracles that Jesus did and out of all the multitudes that He preached to, the initial number of disciples after His death were about 120 (Acts 1:15).

God has His church participating in His work of bringing others to salvation (Matt. 28:19–20). The increase of the number of disciples since that first Pentecost is a testimony of the greater works that Jesus said we would do through the help that He sends from the Father. The spiritual miracle of conversion from sharing God's word supersedes the physical miracles like that of healing. Psalm73:28 says, "But it is good for me to draw near to God; I have put my trust in the Lord God, that I may declare all Your works." Matthew 8:26 states that Jesus calmed the sea, and I can testify to the peace he has given me.

When we look at the history of tithing, its origins can be traced back to the most ancient empires. Ancient Babylonian texts record the custom of tithing for the support of kings and for the building of empires. Genesis 10:8 refers to Nimrod, who began to be a mighty one on the earth. Nimrod was a king, since you cannot have a kingdom without a king. Genesis 10:10 says, "And the beginning of his kingdom was Babel, Erech, Accad and Calneh in the land of Shinar." Shinar, which was Babylonia, was in modern Iraq. Mighty ones or kings became mightier or wealthier by receiving tithes, taxes, or tribute from the weaker inhabitants of the land.

In man's government originating from Babylon, the weak often support the mighty but under God's government it is the strong or mighty who are to support the weak. The Israelite landowners sharing tithes with the nonlandowners, which included the widows, fathers, strangers, and bond servants, depicts God's way of the strong supporting the weak or poor. Ownership of land reflected a source of wealth among ancient Israel and the nonlandowners were typically the poor at that time.

Sadly, many church members who are poor or struggling financially feel obligated to pay monetary tithes to support ministers with lucrative salaries. The early new covenant church ministry was not a paid profession but a sacrificial service supported by offerings. God's church has not completely come out of Babylon, which is why in Revelation 18:4 God says, "Come out of her my people." God's people are the church of God.

Paul worked while preaching the gospel to support himself and those with him (Acts 20:34–35). Paul set the biblical example of the strong supporting the weak. Paul said in Acts 20:35, "I have shown you in every way by laboring like this, that you must support the weak." Romans 11:18 says, "Remember that you do not support the root, but the root supports you." Jesus is the root of David who supports us (Rev. 5:5).

Revelation 22:16 says, "I, Jesus, have sent My angel to testify to you these things in the churches. I am the Root and the Offspring of David, the bright and Morning Star." Romans 15:12 states that Jesus is "a root of Jesse who shall rise to reign over the Gentiles." First John 4:8 says, "He who does not love does not know God, for God is love." Ephesians 3:17 talks about "being rooted and grounded in love." Colossians 2:6 tells us that we are rooted and built up in Christ. Matthew 13:20–21 reveals that those who have no root will stumble when tribulation and persecution arise because of the word. The deeper the root, the harder it is to extract.

First Corinthians 3:11 affirms that Jesus is the foundation that supports God's building—the church or temple of God. Revelation 3:12 talks about "He who overcomes" will be made a pillar in the temple of God. The job of a pillar is to give support. First Thessalonians 5:14 says, "Now we exhort you brethren, warn those who are unruly, comfort the fainthearted, uphold (support) the weak, be patient with all." Jesus is not just the cornerstone that starts and supports the building, but He is also the headstone or capstone that completes the building (Zech. 4:7, Ps. 118:22, Mark 12:10). Jesus being the chief cornerstone or capstone confirms that He is "the Alpha and Omega the Beginning and the End" (Rev. 1:8). Hebrews 12:2 talks about Jesus being "the author and finisher of our faith." Hebrews 12:2 may be interpreted that Jesus is the originator and completer of our faith.

3

THE NEW COVENANT

The law of Moses required a tithe of crops and specific farm animals as a part of the inheritance for the Levites. The inheritance of the new covenant goes way beyond what the law offered. We should realize that we cannot use or change the lucid old covenant ordinance of tithing to enforce monetary tithing under the new covenant. We need to examine the new covenant scriptures to see what the new covenant teaches concerning tithing.

John 10:35 says, "Scripture cannot be broken," which also means the scriptures cannot be altered. To change the tithing laws of the old covenant is a violation of the law and is contrary to the Word of God. Deuteronomy 4:2 says, "You shall not add to the word" which God commanded, "nor take from it." When preachers quote Deuteronomy 14:22 and say, "you shall tithe all the increase" and do not complete the verse, they take away from God's word where it says to "tithe all the increase of your grain that the field produces year by year." If some say to "tithe all the increase of your monetary income," then they are adding to God's word. Adding to God's word or taking away from God's word are ways that false prophets deceive people, especially when it comes to taking their money.

Satan was the first to add to God's word in Genesis 3:4. Satan deceived Eve by just adding one word to what God said in Genesis 2:17. God said in Genesis 2:17, "you shall surely die." Satan said to

Eve in Genesis 3:4, "You shall not surely die." Satan's lies also offer benefits to entice (Gen. 3:5). Men entice people to tithe money by telling them that God will bless them if they tithe, but the blessings that come from God are not based on supporting false doctrines, which may be why many people tithe and still struggle financially.

Some people tithe to support false churches that teach partial truth but not the true gospel. Usually a few from these often large churches may claim that they received physical blessings when they tithed, but the reality is that many people who do not tithe are blessed with material wealth, and many people tithe and still struggle financially. Paul talked about those among the church who distorted the gospel of Christ (Gal. 1:6–12). Changing God's law and peddling the Word were some of the ways that some wanted to pervert the gospel.

Amos 4:14 talks about how Israel departed from God and brought the agrarian tithes to Bethel and Gilgal where false religion was being practiced. God did not bless or approve of this activity. Amos 4:7 mentions that God withheld rain from the people but allowed one part to be rained upon. Matthew 5:45 states: "He makes His sun rise on the evil and on the good, and sends rain on the just and on the unjust." Luke 6:35 reveals that God "is kind to the unthankful and evil." Luke 6:36 says, "Therefore be merciful, just as your Father also is merciful."

Psalms 73 and 37 are scriptures that reveal how even the ungodly increase in wealth and prosper. False prophets want people to believe that if they pay tithes to support them and the church organization then they will be blessed, but many have found out from experience that paying monetary tithes does not necessarily bring blessings. Paying monetary tithes has caused additional stress and problems for some people instead of blessings.

Just because a person or organization is prospering does not mean that God is pleased with what is going on. The church of the Laodiceans described themselves in Revelation 3:17 as, "I am rich, have become wealthy, and have need of nothing." Despite their wealth, God described their spiritual state as "wretched, miserable, poor, blind and naked." God allowed the church of God in the early eighties to be prosperous with college campuses and multimillion-dollar buildings while bringing in an income of around $174 million to well over $224 million a year. Those who know the history of the church of God also know that God allowed this wealth to disappear seemingly almost overnight. Maybe what God says in Proverbs 13:11 was applicable: "Wealth gained by dishonesty will be diminished, but he who gathers by labor will increase."

Many churches of God take the old covenant laws on tithing and change or alter them and then endorse them as if they are part of the new covenant, which is a mistake by which many have been deceived. In Mark 2:22 Jesus said, "and no one puts new wine into old wine-skins." There is a separation between the new and old covenants. There are certain instructions and carnal ordinances under the old covenant, including tithing, that are not applicable to the new covenant.

The history of tithing from a new covenant perspective confirms that the implementation of monetary tithing to finance the church started with the Catholic Church around AD 560 to 585. Various encyclopedias record that tithing was not practiced in the early history of the new covenant church. The new covenant scriptures starting with the book of Acts reveal that ministers and members were supported by voluntary gifts or contributions but not by monetary tithes.

The Book of Acts

The book of Acts gives a record of the beginning of the new covenant church and the faith that was once delivered as Jude 3 tells us to contend earnestly for. The apostles' doctrine did not include the paying of monetary tithes to support them. This would have been a new teaching involving a different type of tithe to a different group besides the Levites. If a new or different doctrine of tithing had occurred in the early church, it would have been recorded somewhere in the new covenant writings.

The teaching and examples of sharing, freely giving, alms giving, contributions, dedicating items, giving offering, and giving hospitality are the examples mentioned in the book of Acts. Sharing or freely giving is reiterated throughout the epistles of the new covenant to support the church and ministry. The philanthropy of the early church involved donating money, food, property, and work to support the needy. From the books of Acts to Revelation there is no evidence that monetary tithing was a practice or doctrine of the church.

Acts 2:44–45 says, "Now all who believed were together and had all things in common, and sold their possessions and goods and divided them among all, as anyone had need." Acts 4:32 says, "Now the multitude of those who believed were of one heart and soul; neither did anyone say that any of the things he possessed was his own, but they had all things in common." Acts 4:34–35 says, "Nor was there anyone among them who lacked; for all who were possessors of lands or houses sold them, and brought the proceeds of the things that were sold, and laid them at the apostles feet; and they distributed to each as anyone had need." Acts chapters 2 and 4 reveal how the early church applied what Jesus said in Luke 12:33: "Sell what you have and give alms." Jesus did not say sell what you have and pay tithes.

Acts chapters 2 and 4 show that the supporting of members and ministry was by sharing and not by the paying of tithes of any kind in the early church. These verses reflect what fellowshipping is about, which few seem to understand today. Fellowship is a partnership of sharing. The donations that were freely given in the early church were used for the needs of the saints. Romans 12:9 says, "Let love be without hypocrisy." This love involves Romans 12:13: "distributing to the needs of the saints, given to hospitality." Acts 4:36–37 says that Barnabas, a Levite, sold land and brought the money to the apostles to distribute to the needy. These verses connote that a new system of giving was implemented and that the apostles instead of the Levites were the overseers in the new covenant church.

The Book of Hebrews
The book of Hebrews mentions more about tithing than any other book of the new covenant. Some try to use this book to confirm that

tithing is a teaching of the new covenant, but Hebrews corroborates the fact that tithing was only an edict for the old covenant. Hebrews 7:5 says, "And indeed those who are of the sons of Levi who receive the priesthood have a commandment to receive tithes from the people according to the law." The words "according to the law" confirm that the law was not disregarded. According to the law meant that tithes were agrarian and not monetary as Leviticus 27:30; Deuteronomy 14:22; Nehemiah 10:37, 12:44; and other scriptures confirm.

The new covenant teaches in the book of Hebrews that the Levites have a commandment to receive tithes. There are no other new covenant instructions for anyone else besides the Levites to receive tithes. In Hebrews 7:5 the words "according to the law" also meant that to pay tithes to any other tribe instead of the Levites would have been a violation of the law. Isaiah warns that those who contradict God's law are in the dark. Isaiah 8:20 says, "To the law and to the testimony! If they do not speak according to this word, it is because there is no light in them."

The two tablets of stone were the testimony or witness of the work of God (Exod. 31:18). When James 1:25 talks about being "a doer of the work," this involves continuing in "the perfect law of liberty." Exodus 32:16 says, "Now the tablets were the work of God, and the writing was the writing of God engraved on the tablets." Deuteronomy 32:4 says, "He is the Rock, His work is perfect; For all His ways are justice, a God of truth and without injustice; Righteous and upright is He." Second Samuel 22:31 says, "As for God His way is perfect." James 1:25 reveals that the doers of the work "will be blessed in what he does."

Hebrews 7:9 says, "even Levi who receives tithes (present tense) paid tithes through Abraham, so to speak." When the book of Hebrews was written the temple had not yet been destroyed so the Levites were still receiving the agrarian tithes for their service of the temple. Hebrews 7:9 is making the point that the Levitical priesthood was inferior to Melchizedek, the king of Salem. Hebrews 7:7 confirms that Levi is the one who is being blessed by Melchizedek. In man's government, the lesser pays to the greater, but in the case of

Melchizedek, the greater or stronger is blessing the lesser or weaker. Melchizedek, the priest of God, pronounced a blessing on Abram in Genesis 14:20 that involved delivering his enemies into his hand.

Hebrews 7:11 says, "Therefore if perfection were through the Levitical priesthood (for under it the people received the law) what further need was there that another priest should rise according to the order of Melchizedek and not be called according to the order of Aaron." This verse says the people received the law under the Levitical priesthood, which was the law that was added because of sin (Gal. 3:19). Hebrews 7:11 is not talking about the royal law or Ten Commandments since when God gave Israel the Ten Commandments in Exodus 20 there was not a Levitical priesthood established at that time. Exodus 40:2–17 reveals that Moses anointed Aaron to minister for God as a priest about one year after the exodus. This event took place about nine months after God spoke the Ten Commandments at Mount Sinai. The law that was added under the Levitical priesthood included God's instructions for tithes, offerings, and sacrifices (Jer. 7:22, Lev. 27:30–32, Deut. 29:1, Gal. 3:19). The Levitical priesthood according to the order of Aaron was the priesthood under the law that is not applicable to the new covenant (Heb. 7:28). The initial covenant God made with Israel is covered in Exodus 20:1 through Exodus 24:8. In the third month of the first year after the exodus, God made a covenant with Israel at Sinai where they heard the voice of the Lord (Deut. 5:24–25). Israel heard the voice of Jesus, who was the spiritual Rock that accompanied them (1 Cor. 10:4). Jesus also confirmed that He was "I AM" (John 8:58). I AM is the name by which the God of the old covenant revealed Himself to Moses (Exod. 3:14). After the second year of the exodus God added various laws or requirements, which included the books of Leviticus and Numbers. In the fortieth year after the exodus God added even more laws, statutes, and judgments for Israel to observe in the land that they were about to possess (Deut. 6:1).

Deuteronomy means the second giving of the law, and this book also included more instructions for the old covenant. In Deuteronomy

5 Moses also reviews the Ten Commandments that God made with Israel at Sinai almost forty years ago. A new generation was preparing to enter the land of Canaan. The "Deuteronomy" was given to remind this generation of the law that God gave at Mount Sinai (Deut. 5:1–22). In the book of Deuteronomy additional tithing laws were implemented besides the original tithing laws that God gave Israel in Leviticus 27 about thirty-nine years earlier.

When a covenant is confirmed it is considered irrevocable and unchangeable, and this principle is addressed in Galatians 3:15. The old covenant that was established for physical Israel included additional laws besides the law of righteousness and was confirmed at Moab by God and Israel just prior to crossing the Jordan (Deut. 26:16–18, 31:26). Deuteronomy 29:1 says, "These are the words of the covenant which the Lord commanded Moses to make with the children of Israel in the land of Moab, besides (in addition to) the covenant which He made with them in Horeb." Horeb means desert and was a reference to Sinai.

The law contained commandments, statutes, and judgments (Deut. 30:16). Israel was to "carefully observe all the words of this law" (Deut. 31:12). The letter of the law included all that was written and declared through Moses (Deut. 27:8–10, Gal. 5:3). The whole letter of the law was to be meticulously observed under the old covenant (Deut. 26:16–17). The Ten Commandments, also called the Decalogue, which James 1:25 refers to as "the perfect law of liberty" was already obligatory. James 2:8 mentions the "royal law," which is also the law of love that existed before God added the law through Moses (Gal. 3:19, John 1:17).

The old covenant that God made with physical Israel also included civil laws, inheritance laws, ceremonial laws, temple laws, Leviticus laws, and other fleshly ordinances. The fleshly ordinances mentioned in Hebrews 9:10 involved food and drink. Under the law of Moses, tithes and sacrifices consisted of food and drink. Fleshly ordinances were "imposed until the time of reformation." The new covenant, which occurred with the death and resurrection of our Lord Jesus Christ, brought about a reformation.

The oldness of the letter of the law is no longer imposed on those who are Jews inwardly. Romans 2:29 says, "but he is a Jew who is one inwardly; and circumcision is that of the heart, in the Spirit, not in the letter; whose praise is not from men but from God." When we have Jesus, who was a Jew, in us then we are Jews inwardly. The spiritual Jews are the spiritual covenant people and the people of the promise by faith (Rom. 4:16, Gal. 3:22). Those who are Christ's are also the spiritual seed of Abraham (Gal. 3:29).

The main point that Hebrews chapter 7 is making is mentioned in the next chapter. Hebrews 8:1 says, "We have such a High Priest who is seated at the right hand of the throne of the Majesty in the heavens." Jesus is a minister of the heavenly sanctuary so we are no longer under the physical Levitical priesthood. We are not required to worship God in a physical earthly temple with its physical ordinances. Concerning the new covenant, Jesus taught in John 4:21–24 that "true worshipers will worship the Father in spirit and truth; for the Father is seeking such to worship Him." Worshiping God in spirit and truth negates the need to go to Jerusalem to worship God in the physical temple with all the ceremonial, symbolic, ritualistic, and carnal ordinances.

Through Jesus our High Priest we have access to the throne of God in heaven. Jesus is our Minister who serves us out of love (Heb. 8:2). Jesus is the way unto the Father as John 14:6 confirms. Hebrews 4:14–16 says, "Seeing then that we have a great High Priest who has passed through the heavens, Jesus the Son of God, let us hold fast our confession. For we do not have a High Priest who cannot sympathize with our weaknesses, but was in all points tempted as we are, yet without sin. Let us therefore come boldly to the throne of grace, that we may obtain mercy and find grace to help in time of need."

Our High Priest is of the tribe of Judah, which means praise. Hebrews concludes that the sacrifice of praise is the sacrifice that we offer now. Instead of offering the fruit of the land, we now offer the fruit of our lips. Hebrews 13:15 says, "Therefore by Him let us continually offer the sacrifice of praise to God, that is the fruit of our lips, giving thanks to His name." Praising and giving thanks to God are spiritual sacrifices that will last forever as we worship our almighty, wonderful, merciful, majestic, awesome, perfect, unlimited, eternal, most high God.

4

THE CROSS

First Corinthians 1:18 says, "For the message of the cross is foolishness to those who are perishing, but to us who are being saved it is the power of God." God has the power to wash away our sins through the cross with the shedding of the blood of Jesus. The penalty of having to keep the law that was added because of sin was nailed to the cross. Colossians 2:14 says, "having wiped out the handwriting of requirements that was against us, which was contrary to us, And He has taken it out of the way, having nailed it to the cross." What was added to the way because of sin was taken out of the way because of the remission of sin through the cross, or atoning sacrifice, of our Savior.

The book of the law containing additional requirements was a witness against Israel testifying to their rebellion (Deut. 31:27). Deuteronomy 31:26 says, "Take this Book of the Law and put it beside the ark of the covenant of the Lord your God, that it may be there as a witness against you." Our record of indebtedness involved keeping the whole letter of the law until Jesus paid the penalty for our sins. Jesus delivered us from the letter of the law and redeemed us from the curse of the law (Rom. 7:6, Gal 3:13).

The message of the cross is a message of the victory of our Savior over the devil. The message of the cross is a message of the sacrificial love of God. John 3:16 says, "For God so loved the world that He gave His only begotten Son, that whoever believes in Him should not perish but have everlasting life." The message of the cross is a message about the greatest love of all. John 15:13 says, "Greater love has no one than this, than to lay down one's life for his friends." To be a friend of Jesus is such an awesome blessing. Jesus said in John 15:14: "You are My friends if you do whatever I command you."

The old covenant carnal ordinances associated with the physical temple that was destroyed in 70 AD are no longer imposed on us who are the temple of God today. Colossians 2:16 says, "So let no one judge you in food or in drink, or regarding a festival or new moon or Sabbaths." God's festivals or Sabbaths are not done away with under the new covenant, but we no longer keep these festivals according to the letter of the law with all the celebratory food and drink. The food and drink ordinances of the old covenant consisted of tithes, libations, and animal sacrifices offered on the new moons and holy days. We no longer are required to keep the whole letter of the law with all the temple rituals and added ordinances with all the physical feasting.

Under the law, the holy days offerings were "made by fire" as mentioned in various scriptures such as Leviticus 23:8. The burnt offerings were for God alone and signified total consecration and dedication to the Lord. Other types of offerings were shared with the one offering it and the priests. Under the new covenant Hebrews 13:10 says, "We have an altar from which those who serve the tabernacle (under the old covenant) have no right to eat." Hebrews 13:13 reveals that one must spiritually come "outside the camp" to eat of the spiritual altar. The camp would be the earthly Jerusalem, which was still in bondage under the law (Gal. 4:25). We have been delivered from the old covenant to worship God in the newness of the Spirit. Under the new covenant we partake of the altar that represents the sacrifice of Christ. We are now blessed to partake of the altar that symbolizes our fellowship with Christ, which also involves partaking of His righteousness. Under the new covenant we can offer an offering made by fire, but we do not need the physical fire used on the altar in the old covenant. When we offer ourselves to

God as a living sacrifice, we are prepared with a different type of fire. Mark 9:49 says, "For everyone will be seasoned with fire, and every sacrifice will be seasoned with salt." Fire symbolizes various things. In Exodus chapter 3 the burning bush showed how fire symbolized the presence of God. Fire also symbolizes light; fire symbolizes being hot or zealous for God, and fire symbolizes being purified or refined. The fiery trials are a test of our faith that will result in praise, honor, and glory at the revelation of Jesus Christ. Making it through the fire or trial by trusting in God proves the genuineness of our faith (1 Pet. 1:7).

Shadrach, Meshach, and Abednego were cast into the burning fiery furnace for not worshiping the golden image that the king of Babylon set up. When we go through our fiery trial, we can have the solace of knowing that our Savior is with us as He was with Shadrach, Meshach, and Abednego (Dan. 3:25). These men experienced deliverance from their fiery trial because they trusted in God (Dan. 3:24–28). The tongues as of fire that appeared on Pentecost revealed that the Spirit gave the disciples inspired speech (Acts 2:3–4). Mark 9:49 also mentions that we are seasoned with salt, which represents something that will not spoil.

Ephesians 2:14 talks about the "middle wall" alluding to the temple being broken down that separated Jews from Gentiles. Ephesians 2:15 says, "having abolished in His flesh the enmity, that is the law of commandments contained in ordinances, so as to create in Himself one new man from the two, thus making peace." The death of Jesus brought about a new covenant void of the Levitical and ceremonial ordinances. These ordinances would also include the tithing laws, which is why we do not tithe according to the law of Moses under the new covenant.

Ephesians 2:16 says, "and that He might reconcile them both to God in one body through the cross." Jews and Gentiles are to be partakers of the one body and of the bread and wine of the new covenant. Ephesians 2:18 says, "For through Him (Jesus) we both have access by one Spirit to the Father." All Christians have a communion, fellowship, or portion of the same Spirit (2 Cor. 13:14).

What an awesome blessing it is to have access to the Father and to be a part of the household of faith.

Hebrews 10:20 mentions the "new and living way which He (Jesus) consecrated for us through the veil, that is His flesh." When Jesus died on the cross, as Matthew 27:51 says, "Then behold, the veil of the temple was torn in two from top to bottom." This event symbolized the new and living way that Jesus opened up for us as we serve and worship God in the Spirit. Romans 8:3–4 says that Jesus condemned sin in the flesh "that the righteous requirement of the law might be fulfilled in us who do not walk according to the flesh but according to the Spirit." The righteous requirement of the law, the Decalogue—the moral law of love—was not abrogated through the cross of Christ, but this spiritual law is subsumed under the new covenant.

Colossians 2:15 reveals more of what Jesus did through the cross, "Having disarmed principalities and powers," He took away Satan's power to condemn us and keep us under the bondage of the law (Gal. 5:1, 4:25, 5:18). Jesus was triumphant over the powers of darkness on the cross. Hebrews 2:14–15 says, "Inasmuch then as the children have partaken of flesh and blood, He Himself likewise shared in the same, that through death He might destroy him who had the power of death, that is the devil, and release those who through fear of death were all their lifetime subject to bondage." Our Jesus went from life to death so that we could go from death to life. The message of the cross is a message of liberation.

The cross of Jesus is also a message of the destruction of Satan. John 3:14 says, "And as Moses lifted up the serpent in the wilderness, even so must the Son of Man be lifted up." Moses lifting the serpent on the pole in Numbers 21:8–9 was a prophetic message of the lifting of Jesus. When Jesus was lifted on the cross it was the serpent, or devil, that was being destroyed. In John 12:32 Jesus said, "And I, if I am lifted up from the earth, will draw all peoples to Myself." Through the lifting of Christ on the cross, we can be drawn to our Savior. The altar was a place for sacrifice (Matt. 5:23–24). The cross became the altar that altered the way we serve God (Rom. 7:6).

The devil destroys by deceiving and influencing people to sin. First John 5:19 says, "We know that we are of God, and the whole world lies under the sway of the wicked one." Jesus put away sin by the sacrifice of Himself (Heb. 9:26). Through the cross of Christ, we have been extricated from sin, and we shall be saved by His life, according to Romans 5:10. In John 14:19 Jesus said, "Because I live, you will live also." The perfect life of Yeshua as a Lamb without blemish qualified Him to be our atoning sacrifice (1 John 4:10, Heb. 4:15). The life of Jesus Christ as our High Priest making propitiation or conciliation for our sins enables us to be saved.

For us to have salvation we need the forgiveness of sins. Hebrews 9:22 says, "without the shedding of blood there is no remission or forgiveness." Leviticus 17:11 says, "For the life of the flesh is in the blood, and I have given it to you upon the altar to make atonement for your souls, it is the blood that makes atonement for your soul." Christ shed His life or blood so that we could be saved by His life. The shedding of the blood of goats and calves could only make one ceremonially clean under the old covenant (Heb. 9:13). Hebrews 9:14–15 says, "How much more shall the blood of Christ, who through the eternal Spirit offered Himself without spot to God, cleanse your conscience from dead works to serve the living God? And for this reason, He is the Mediator of the new covenant, that those who are called may receive the promise of the eternal inheritance."

Our High Priest aids us who are tempted (Heb. 2:16–18). Having Christ living in us enables us to be saved by His life. Hebrews 7:25 says, "Therefore He (Jesus) is also able to save to the uttermost those who come to God through Him, since He always lives to make intercession for them." Jesus grants us aid, forgiveness, mercy, and grace as our High Priest and gives us access to the Father (John 14:6). First John 2:1 says, "We have an Advocate with the Father, Jesus Christ the righteous." Hebrews 3:1 states: "Therefore, holy brethren, partakers of the heavenly calling, consider the Apostle and High Priest of our confession, Christ Jesus." Hebrews 13:6 says, "The Lord is my helper." Mark 8:34 says, "When He had called the people to Himself, with His disciples also, He said to them, 'Whoever desires to come after Me, let him deny himself, and take up his cross, and follow Me.'" To follow Christ, we need to deny the self. The cross is a symbol of death, and it is the old self, which is selfish, that needs to die. The more we allow Christ to live in us through the power of the Holy Spirit, the more we will deny our self. Romans 8:13 says, "For if you live according to the flesh you will die; but if by the Spirit you put to death the deeds of the body, you will live."

We are to live for our Savior and not for our self. Second Corinthians 5:15 says, "And He died for all, that those who live should live no longer for themselves, but for Him who died for them and rose again." Luke 20:38 says, "For He is not the God of the dead but of the living, for all live to Him." We should live like the burning bush mentioned in Exodus 3:2 and be on fire for the Lord. Without a zeal for God we die. Revelation 3:19 says, "As many as I love, I rebuke and chasten. Therefore, be zealous and repent."

We are witnesses of the resurrection of Christ by allowing Him to live in us. Acts 5:30–32 says, "The God of our fathers raised up Jesus whom you murdered by hanging on a tree. Him God has exalted to His right hand to be Prince and Savior, to give repentance to Israel and forgiveness of sins. And we are His witnesses to these things and so also is the Holy Spirit whom God has given to those who obey Him." The sending of the Holy Spirit by Jesus confirms that He ascended to the Father and is our Mediator (John 15:26, Heb. 12:24). The Spirit imparts the divine nature of God (2 Pet. 1:4). Romans 8:16 says, "The Spirit Himself bears witness with our spirit that we are children of God." The testimony of two gives a witness validity (John 8:17).

John 19:17 says, "And He bearing His cross, went out to a place called the place of a Skull, which is called in Hebrew Golgotha, where they crucified Him." What Jesus went through and suffered for our sake at Calvary took the power of God. For us to take up our cross and follow Christ requires the power of God. The message of the cross is a message of the power of God. The gospel of Christ is "the power of God to salvation for everyone who believes" (Rom. 1:16). The transformation or conversion process that we go through involves putting off the old man and putting on the new according to Ephesians 4:22–24. Colossians 3:9–10 says, "Do not lie to one another, since you have put off the old man with his deeds, and have put on the new man who is renewed in knowledge according to the image of Him who created him." The knowledge of the Word and being partakers of the Holy Spirit enlightens us. Repentance involves putting on the new man or being renewed (Heb. 6:6). Galatians 3:27 says, "For as many of you as have been baptized into Christ have put on Christ."

Not Under the Law

Romans 8:1–2 confirms that we are not under the condemnation of the law. Romans 3:20–21 reveals that we are not under the law for obtaining righteousness like the legalistic righteousness of the scribes and Pharisees. Galatians 4:21–26 and Galatians 5:3–4 reveal that we are not under the old covenant or the whole Mosaic law, which is why physical circumcision is not required for Gentile believers. The temple and Leviticus ordinances are not a part of the new covenant. The old covenant Leviticus tithing laws are not applicable to the new covenant; if they were, we would be still tithing crops and animals according to the law. God assigned certain temple tasks solely for the Levites. These tasks excluded them from the farming occupation of Israel. Romans 7:6 reveals that we are delivered from the letter of the law which involved temple ordinances. The Torah and Talmud contain written regulations that were exclusively for physical Israel. Proselytism was allowed under certain circumstances for those that were of non-Israelite descent.

No man can change God's laws, but Romans 7:6 says, "We have been delivered from the law … so that we should serve in the newness of the spirit and not in the oldness of the letter." In 2 Corinthians 3:6 Paul says, "who also made us sufficient as ministers of the new covenant, not of the letter but of the spirit, for the letter kills, but the spirit gives life." Under the letter of the law, the death penalty and stoning were enforced for major infractions. We do not want to be under the letter of the law since "the letter kills." The sacrifices and burnt offerings offered according to the law could never take away sin (Heb. 10:11). Animal sacrifices reiterated the fact that the wages of sin is death under the letter of the law.

Romans 8:2 says, "For the law of the Spirit of life in Christ Jesus has made me free from the law of sin and death." The law of sin and death was enforced under the old covenant. The letter of the law could not produce eternal life. Under the law according to Romans 6:23, "the wages of sin is death" (originating with Adam and Eve in Genesis 2:17), "but the gift of God is eternal life in Christ Jesus our Lord." The word *gift* literally means free gift. Jesus is the second Adam, which "became a life giving Spirit" (1 Cor. 15:45).

The death and resurrection of Jesus brought about a reformation and change in the way we serve God, which requires God's Spirit. Hebrews 7:12 states: "the priesthood being changed of necessity there is also a change of the law." The change of the law is *not* a change *in* the law. The change of the law is a change from the law, since Jesus has delivered us from the law according to Romans 7:6. Hebrews 7:18 says, "There is an annulling of the former commandment." This is talking about the law of a fleshly commandment involving the genealogy of Levi. Under the new covenant we no longer adhere to all the laws pertaining to the Levitical priesthood since our High Priest is of the tribe of Judah.

The book of Hebrews and other scriptures also reveal that there is no change in the law but a change from the law, which is why Hebrews 7:5 says that the sons of Levi "have a commandment to receive tithes from the people according to the Law." The old covenant was still practiced by the physical Jews who had not accepted Christ and His sacrifice and had not come into the new covenant. God will eventually make the new covenant in the future with the physical house of Israel and Judah according to Hebrews 8:8–10 and Jeremiah 31:33. The new covenant church is not the house of Israel or Judah, but the church today is the house of God (Heb. 10:21). First Timothy 3:15 says, "the house of God which is the church of the living God, the pillar and ground of the truth."

The church today is comprised of all different nationalities and types of people. Matthew 13:47 reveals how God is gathering "some of every kind." The church is also referred to as a holy nation in 1 Peter 2:9. The old covenant was with the physical nation of Israel, but the new covenant is with spiritual Israel. Galatians 6:16 confirms that the new creation includes "the Israel of God." The Israel of God are the servants of God. Isaiah 44:21 states: "And Israel, for you are my servant; I have formed you, you are My servant." Isaiah 61:6 says, "But you shall be named the priests of the Lord, They shall call you the servants of our God." Throughout the Bible there is a duality principle with the physical and the spiritual aspect of things. Second Timothy 2:24 says, "And a servant of the Lord must not quarrel but be gentle to all, able to teach, patient."

First Peter 2:9 refers to the church as a "chosen generation." The chosen few and elect are all the same generation going back to Able, Enoch, Noah, Abraham, and others, to those living in this end-time because we will all be born again in the first resurrection. Revelation 20:6 says, "Blessed and holy is he who has part in the first resurrection, over such the second death has no power, but they shall be priests of God and of Christ, and shall reign with Him a thousand years."

Jeremiah 2:3 says, "Israel was holiness to the Lord, the first-fruits of His increase." Revelation 7:4–8 is a reference to physical Israel who will be sealed for protection during the time of tribulation. The spiritual Israel is mentioned in Revelation 14, which is the new covenant church. Revelation 14:4 says, "These were redeemed from among men, being first fruits to God and to the Lamb." James 1:18 says, "Of His own will He brought us forth by the word of truth, that we might be a kind of first fruits of His creatures."

The first fruits to God and to the Lord are those who are chosen to reign with Christ at His return (Rev. 5:10, 20:5). Pentecost symbolizes the first harvest of the first fruits (Exod. 34:22). Fifty is the number that symbolizes freedom. The Jubilee year was the fiftieth year when slaves were freed, and debts were released (Lev. 25:10–17). The counting of fifty days (Lev. 23:16) symbolizes the freedom that God offers us under the new covenant. The perfect law of liberty was promulgated on the day of Pentecost. Second Corinthians 3:17 says, "where the Spirit of the Lord is, there is liberty."

The Israel of God today are those who wrestle with God against spiritual wickedness. When Jacob wrestled with God he would not let go until he was blessed, according to Genesis 32:26–30. Israel means one who prevails with God. As spiritual Israel we must hold on to God as we wrestle spiritually. Ephesians 6:12 says, "For we do not wrestle against flesh and blood, but against principalities, against powers, against the rulers of the darkness of this age, against spiritual hosts of wickedness in heavenly places." As we grapple spiritually, we need to put on the whole armor of God to stand and prevail with God. When it comes to Christ, Romans 8:37 says, "We are more than conquerors through Him who loved us."

The armor of God involves truth, righteousness, the gospel of peace, salvation, and the word of God. We need to be praying always with all prayer and supplication in the Spirit. We need to be watchful or alert with perseverance (Eph. 6:13–18). We need to present our request and petitions to God with thanksgivings (Phil. 4:6). Ephesians 5:15–16 says, "See then that you walk circumspectly (carefully) not as fools but as wise, redeeming the time, because the days are evil." Walking circumspectly involves being diligent. We need to "be diligent to make our call and election sure" (2 Pet. 1:10).

Second Corinthians 3:18 reveals that we go "from glory to glory." From the glory of the old covenant, which is passing away, or transitory, to the glory of the new covenant, which remains glorious (2 Cor. 3:11). In 2 Corinthians 3:7–10 Paul does not depreciate the law that reflects the will and way of God. What was written and engraved on stones by God needs to be engrafted or implanted in our hearts. James 1:21 says, "Therefore lay aside all filthiness and receive with meekness the implanted word, which is able to save your souls." Through the power of the Holy Spirit the spiritual law of love is written on our hearts (Heb. 8:10). Romans 8:2 says, "For the law of the Spirit of life in Christ Jesus has made us free from the law of sin and death."

Our Deliverer delivered us from the legalism of the letter of the law and introduced a better covenant (Heb. 8:6). Romans 11:26–27 says, "The Deliverer will come out of Zion, and He will turn away ungodliness from Jacob; For this is My covenant with them, when I take away their sins." Colossians 1:13 says, "He has delivered us from the power of darkness and conveyed us into the kingdom of the Son of His love." Mark 4:26–29 is a parable that reveals how the kingdom of God comes in stages before the harvest. The church is in the embryonic stage of the kingdom prior to Christ's return.

Our Lord delivers us from darkness to light and from the power of Satan to God (Acts 26:18). Psalm 37:40 says, "And the Lord shall help them and deliver them from the wicked, and save them, because they trust in Him." God manumits us from the spirit of bondage, which is the spirit of this world. First Corinthians 2:12 says, "Now we have received, not the spirit of the world, but the Spirit which is from God, that we might know the things that have been freely given to us by God." What has been freely given to us by God does not require paying a tithe.

First Timothy 1:8 says, "But we know that the law is good if one uses it lawfully." We should use the law to get sound doctrine, but if we change what is written then that is not using the law lawfully. Jesus said to the Jews who sought to kill Him in John 5:46–47: "for if you believed Moses, you would believe Me; for he wrote about Me. But if you do not believe his writings, how will you believe My words?" The words of Jesus did not contradict the law. What Jesus taught did not deviate from the writings of Moses, unlike what men teach about tithing.

The change of or from the law involves not being under the Levitical priesthood since our High Priest is of the tribe of Judah instead of Levi. If Jesus had come from the tribe of Levi, the Leviticus laws would have applied to Jesus, and this would not have been a new priesthood, nor would this have been a change from the law. An important point to understand about the book of Hebrews along with the rest of the new covenant scriptures is that they do not address any changes to the tithing laws. The change in the tithing laws from agrarian to monetary came by the commandments of men and not by the Word of God. False teachers also changed the tithing laws from being an inheritance for the Levites to being a means for paying hirelings.

The new covenant scriptures do not implement any new tithing laws. The eight times that tithing is mentioned in the new covenant is always in reference to the old covenant, or Pentateuch. The term *tithe* is never used in the Bible to support the new covenant ministry of apostles, prophets, teachers, evangelists, laborers, and pastors. The tithe from the land for an inheritance for the Levites under the old covenant has no association with being a means for paying or hiring preachers. First Corinthians 9:14 confirms that those who preach the gospel should be supported by "offerings" from those being blessed with the good news. When 1 Corinthians 9:13–14 mentions "those who preach the gospel" this is not limited to just pastors; evangelists, teachers, and missionaries all have the right to accept support from the offerings of those to whom they minister. Offerings freely offered in whatever amount one chooses is the choice that we have under the new covenant to support laborers as explained throughout the scriptures.

Exodus 16:4 mentions that God fed Israel with manna. He "rained bread from heaven." Deuteronomy 8:3 states that God fed Israel with manna to make them know that "man shall not live by bread alone, but man lives by every word that proceeds from the mouth of the Lord." The Word commanded the manna to come from heaven, so God's word provided Israel with what they needed to live by. The Word provides both the physical and spiritual food.

In Genesis 1:3 the Word spoke creation into existence, and the Word offers us eternal life (John 3:16). John 6:27 says, "Do not labor for the food which perishes, but for the food which endures to everlasting life, which the Son of Man will give you, because God the Father has set His seal on Him." John 6:57–58 reveals that Jesus is the Word that we need to feed on to live forever. We should be voracious for the word which is necessary for life. First Timothy 4:6 talks about being "nourished in the words of faith and of good doctrine." Christ nourishes and cherishes the church (Eph. 5:29). We should carefully ruminate on the good doctrine and reject all false doctrines.

A mistake some have made is that they incorrectly believe that to live by every word that proceeds from the mouth of God means to live by both the old and new covenants. But the books of Hebrews, Galatians, Romans, and many other new covenant scriptures make clear distinctions and major differences between the old and new covenants. Men take the old covenants laws such as tithing and alter or fabricate them and try to make them applicable to the new covenant. Those who include money as a tithing requirement are adding on to what we are warned not to add on to in Deuteronomy 4:2 and 12:32. Proverbs 30:5–6 states: "Every word of God is pure; He is a shield to those who put their trust in Him. Do not add to His words, lest He rebuke you, and you be found a liar." Given that, it does not require paying money to receive this gift, but it does require faith. Since what most churches teach about tithing does not agree with the Word of God, it is not a matter of true faith, which is the faith of Jesus. Through faith we do not make changes to the law, but we establish the law (Rom. 3:31). Faith corresponds with the law.

The faith of Abraham preceded the old covenant law. Galatians 3:24–25 says, "Therefore the law was our tutor to bring us to Christ, that we might be justified by faith. But after faith has come, we are no longer under a tutor." We have the faith that comes through Christ (Acts 3:16). Instead of being under the tutelage of the law, we have the guidance of the transforming power of the Spirit of faith. Romans 12:2 says, "And do not be conformed to this world, but be transformed by the renewing of your mind." Hebrews 11:1 says, "Now faith is the substance of things hoped for, the evidence of things not seem." Faith gives us confidence and a realization of what is real. We need to hold on to this confidence and rejoice in the hope of glory as a result of Christ in us (Heb. 3:6, Col. 1:27).

Romans 10:17 says, "so then faith comes by hearing, and hearing by the word of God." God through His Spirit enables us to hear and understand and obey His word. We need to be fed the word, the spiritual food, in order to live by faith. Living by faith means living by the word of God. The word is the sword that can circumcise our hearts and ears to hear and receive God's truth into our hearts. The word is a sword that can penetrate beyond the surface. Be a leader by following the Lord, and fight the fight with a spiritual sword.

The word needs to be internalized or inculcated into our hearts. In the book of Acts, Stephen accused the Jews of being stubborn about accepting the truth. Acts 7:51 says, "You stiff-necked and un-circumcised in heart and ears! You always resist the Holy Spirit; as your fathers did, so do you." Israel resisted the prophets who spoke by being led by the Holy Spirit, so they were resisting the Holy Spirit (2 Pet. 1:21).

Romans 1:17 says, "for in it (the gospel) the righteousness of God is revealed from faith to faith. Ephesians 4:5 declares that there is one faith. When we go from faith to faith, it is from the faith of Abraham (Rom. 4:16) to the faith of his seed being Jesus (Gal. 3:16). Rom. 5:5 says, "through whom also we have access by faith into this grace in which we stand, and rejoice in hope of the glory of God." Galatians 3:29 says, "And if you are Christ's then you are Abraham's seed." Romans 9:8 says, "That is those who are the children of the flesh, these are not the children of God; but the children of the promise are counted as the seed." The children of the flesh are the children under the law (Gal. 4:31). Galatians 4:28 says, "Now we brethren as Isaac was, are children of promise." Hebrews 2:16 states that Jesus gives "aid to the seed of Abraham." Jesus is the word of faith preached by God's ministers (Rom. 10:8).

Romans 9:30 says, "What shall we say then? That Gentiles, who did not pursue righteousness, have attained to righteousness, even the righteousness of faith; but Israel pursuing the law of righteousness (Josh. 3:3) has not attained to the law of righteousness. Why? Because they did not seek it by faith, but as it were, by the works of the law. For they stumbled at that stumbling stone." Because of grace through faith we have the gift of righteousness (Rom. 5:15–21). When Romans 5:19 talks about Jesus it says, "by one Man's obedience many will be made righteous." Romans 4:13 says, "For the promise that he would be the heir of the world was not to Abraham or to his seed through the law, but through the righteousness of faith." Romans 3:26 says, "For you are all sons of God through faith in Christ Jesus."

God Gives the Increase

Israel tithed on the increase of the grain that the field produced year by year (Deut. 14:22). A lesson from the law was not only did the land belong to God, but God is the One who gives the increase. God blessed Israel in their increase or produce so that they could feast and rejoice before Him (Deut. 16:15). Colossians 2:19 affirms that we must stay connected to the "Head being Christ from whom all the body is nourished and knit together and grows with the increase that is from God." First Corinthians 3:6–7 reiterates, "but God who gives the increase." All that is produced from the land to sustain humans ultimately comes from God through His Word. God is our Sustainer (Ps. 55:22). We live by the Word which provides. Yahweh-Yireh (Gen. 22:14).

God is not only sharing what he has with humankind; God is also sharing Himself with humans. First John 1:3 says, "Our fellowship is with the Father and with His Son Jesus Christ." Fellowship is a partnership, a participation, a communion, a sharing together, which is what the new covenant exemplifies. The knowledge of fellowshipping with God goes back to even Cain and Able, which is what their offerings represented in Genesis chapter 4. A lesson for us to learn from Cain and Able is that when our works are evil then God does not respect our offering. God said to Cain in Genesis 4:7: "If you do well, will you not be accepted?" When God accepts us then He will also accept what we offer.

If we are not living right and offer prayers to God, then our prayers get rejected. James 5:16 says, "The effective fervent prayer of a righteous man avails much." First Peter 3:12 says, "For the eyes of the Lord are on the righteous, and His ears are open to their prayers; But the face of the Lord is against those who do evil." Jeremiah 6:19–20 talks about how people gave offerings and sacrifices, but they were not accepted by God. Calamity came upon these people because they failed to pay attention to God's words and law. When we pay attention to what the Word says about tithing, it should be evident that this carnal ordinance is only for those under the Levitical priesthood.

The physical mark or omen placed on Cain may remind us of another mark mentioned several times in the book of Revelation. A correlation can be made between the mark placed on Cain and the mark of the beast. The mark placed on Cain was a mark of shame and protection (Gen. 4:15). Revelation 20:4 reveals that the mark of the beast is a mark of protection from persecution which comes to those who do not received his mark. The mark of the beast has to do with false worship. Revelation 15:2 and Revelation 16:2 mention those "who had the mark of the beast and those who worshiped his image."

Cain was the firstborn to start a way or a religion apart from the Way. Genesis 4:16 states: "Then Cain went out from the presence of the Lord (the Way) and dwelt in the land of Nod." Nod means wandering, and any religion or ideology that wanders from John 14:6—"the way, the truth and the life"—is false. All false religion including counterfeit Christianity can fall under the mark of the beast. The mark of the beast involves worship in a wrong way. Jude 11 mentions how some among the church "have gone in the way of Cain."

From the very beginning God desired to have a fellowship with humans starting with Adam and Eve. Genesis 2:16 says, "And the Lord God commanded the man, saying, 'Of every tree of the garden you may freely eat.'" No tithes were required from anyone during the time of Adam and Eve, but the Ten Commandments were enforced at that time. The fourth commandment came about in Genesis 2:3, since the Sabbath was made for humans (Mark 2:27–28).The only thing that God restricted from man was the tree of the knowledge of good and evil (Gen. 2:17).Sadly Adam and Eve chose to experience evil with the influence of the serpent called the devil.

David understood that the sacrifices that God really desires from us are not our physical possessions. Psalm 51:16 says, "For You do not desire sacrifice, or else I would give it; You do not delight in burnt offering." In Matthew 12:7 Jesus said, "I desire mercy and not sacrifice." What God really wants from us is a repentant and humble heart. Psalm 51:17 says, "The sacrifices of God are a broken spirit, A broken and a contrite heart—These, O God, You will not despise." Proverbs 21:3 says, "To do righteousness and justice is more acceptable to the Lord than sacrifice."

In Acts 13:22 David was referred to as a man after God's own heart. Part of what made David a man after God's own heart was his answered prayer in Psalm 51:10 which says, "Create in me a clean heart, O God, And renew a steadfast (right) spirit within me." The Holy Spirit of God enables us to be a man or woman after God's own heart and enables us to be spiritually minded. To be spiritually minded is life and peace (Rom. 8:6). Second Corinthians 2:16 says, "But we have the mind of Christ."

When we serve God in the newness of the Spirit, we do not need to include the carnal ordinances of the old covenant in our worship of God. Malachi 3:7–8 and Hebrews 9:10 reveal that the tithes and offerings associated with the earthly sanctuary of the old covenant were "fleshly ordinances" imposed until the time of the reformation. These ordinances were regulations and procedures incorporated under Judaism (Eph. 2:15). Hebrews 9:11 says, "But Christ came as High Priest of good things to come, with the greater and more perfect tabernacle not made with hands, that is, not of this creation." Genesis 2:7 says, "And the Lord formed man of the dust of the ground." Man came from the earth that belongs to God. We are "God's field," according to 1 Corinthians 3:9. God's seed, being God's word, is planted in us His field to produce spiritual fruit (Gal. 5:22–23). God gives this increase of the fruit of His Spirit. God's Word and God's Spirit are inextricable with the wise servants (Matt. 25:4). In John 6:63 Jesus said, "The words that I speak to you are spirit, and they are life." We need to be wise and make sure we have the oil and the lamp, the Spirit and the Word (Matt. 25:4). When the Word of God is the seed that is planted in us with the power of the Holy Spirit we grow, increase, and abound in love. Mark 4:8 talks about the seed that fell on good ground, which increased and produced a crop. First Thessalonians 3:12 says, "And may the Lord make you increase and abound in love to one another and to all, just as we do to you." The increase that comes from God is unlimited. Isaiah 9:7 says, "Of the increase of His government and peace there will be no end." Because God's increase is endless, we will always have faith and hope in God.

The fruit that we offer to God that comes from us His field under the new covenant is not limited to the physical. The predominant fruit that personifies and glorifies God is the fruit of the Spirit. Galatians 5:22–23 says, "But the fruit of the Spirit is love, joy, peace, long-suffering, kindness, goodness, faithfulness, gentleness, self-control." We also offer the fruit of our lips with thanksgiving and praise (Heb. 13:15). We need Jesus the true vine to be able to bear much fruit. John 15:5 says, "I am the vine, you are the branches. He who abides in Me, and I in him, bears much fruit; for without Me you can do nothing."

The first dictate that God gave to man in Genesis 1:28 was to "be fruitful." Being fruitful includes doing good works (Eph. 2:10). God chose and ordained His church to bear fruit (John 15:16). John 15:17 says, "These things I command you, that you love one another." The sons of God are those who are being led by love (Rom. 8:14). Love is what we receive from God. We need to drink in of the Spirit that God pours out on us. Matthew 5:6 says, "Blessed are those who hunger and thirst for righteousness, for they shall be filled." God wants us to be filled with His Love.

This Love
Love is a blessing that comes from above,
produced from the Spirit of life and love.
This love is holy, harmless, and heavenly;
this love is what God has called us to be.
This love is what the Holy Spirit imparts;
this love is poured out within our hearts.

Joy is a blessing that comes from above,
produced from the Spirit of life and love.
This love is the one that casts out fear;
this love is so certain and so sincere.
This love is free with so much to give;
this love enables us to rejoice and live.

Peace is a blessing that comes from above,
produced from the Spirit of life and love.
This love has beauty beyond any flower;
this love is strong and so full of power.
This love gives grace, and it is a guide;
this love can spread so far and wide.

Long-suffering is a blessing that comes from above,
produced from the Spirit of life and love.
This love is unlimited from the Most High;
this love is for us to show and apply.
This love we know now is not so strange;
this love is spiritual and does not change.

Kindness is a blessing that comes from above,
produced from the Spirit of life and love.
This love is forever and will ever endure;
this love never fails, and this love can cure.
This love promotes us to give God praise;
this love in complete with no end of days.

Goodness is a blessing that comes from above,
produced from the Spirit of life and love.
This love is absolute, and it is so right;
this love is the law of liberty and light.
This love involves being together as one;
this love is why God sacrificed His Son.

Faithfulness is a blessing that comes from above,
produced from the Spirit of life and love.
This love is a treasure we are blessed to find;
this love is a pleasure to keep in mind.
This love abides within God's sheep;
this love is so awesome and so deep.

Gentleness is a blessing that comes from above,
produced from the Spirit of life and love.
This love is incorruptible and supreme;
this love is a gift that we highly esteem.
This love is the way to increase and excel;
this love is from the God of Israel.

Self-control is a blessing that comes from above,
produced from the Spirit of life and love.
This love I have is so great and ideal,
this love I have is so high and real.
This love I have is so serving and true;
this love I have is God's love for you.

And though I have the gift of prophecy, and understand all mysteries and all knowledge; and though I have all faith, so that I could remove mountains, but have not love I am nothing. (1 Corinthians 13:2)

The Royal Priesthood

Jesus is the Christ or Messiah, which means the Anointed One. Jesus was anointed by the Father to be our King and High Priest. Acts 10:38 states: "God anointed Jesus of Nazareth with the Holy Spirit and with power." The Holy Spirit is also the oil of gladness (Heb. 1:9). This word *gladness* in the Greek also means exceeding joy. This joy of the Lord can also be our strength. Regardless of what we go through, we have a reason to rejoice in the Lord. Philippians 4:4 says, "Rejoice in the Lord always. Again I will say, rejoice!"

Jesus our High Priest mentioned part of what He was anointed to do in Luke 4:18–19, which says,

> The Spirit of the Lord is upon Me, Because He has anointed Me to preach the gospel to the poor; He has sent Me to heal the broken hearted, To proclaim liberty to the captives, and recovery of sight to the blind. To set at liberty those who are oppressed; To proclaim the acceptable year of the Lord.

Preaching the gospel to the poor can involve both those who are physically poor and those who are poor in the spirit of this world (Matt. 5:2). The world has a spirit of pride, but God desires for us to have a spirit of humility. Preaching good news to the poor and offering liberty to the oppressed did not include making them pay monetary tithes. The liberty that Jesus proclaimed included deliverance from the old covenant. In Acts 13:38–39, Paul said that "through this Man (Jesus) is preached to you the forgiveness of sins; and by Him everyone who believes is justified from all things from which you could not be justified by the law of Moses."

The liberty of the Lord is from corruption to justification. The new covenant writings reveal that there were poor and needy people in the church. James 2:5 says, "Listen, my beloved brethren; Has God not chosen the poor of this world to be rich in faith and heirs of the kingdom which He promised to those who love Him?" The spiritual prosperity supersedes the physical. Loving God involves keeping His commandments (Exod. 20:6, John 15:10, 1 John 5:3).

All church members of the body of Christ are betrothed to Jesus our High Priest and King, which makes them part of the royal priesthood. This is the priesthood under the new covenant instead of the Levitical priesthood. First Corinthians 6:17 states, "But he who is joined to the Lord is one spirit with Him." When a husband and wife are joined, 1 Corinthians 6:16 says, "the two shall become one flesh." Before the final marriage we go through an engagement or betrothal period. During this testing period we must continue in the faith to actually be the wife of the Lamb. Hebrews 3:14 says, "For we have become partakers of Christ if we hold the beginning of our confidence steadfast to the end."

Levi means joined, and the Levites were joined to Aaron the high priest and his sons under the old covenant. The book of Numbers expounds on the offering of the Levites. The atonement made for the Levites (Num. 8:12–21) had nuptial connotations. Atonement denotes being "at one," which is what marriage depicts. The amalgamation of the Levites with the Aaronic priesthood was a type of the church being joined to Jesus our High Priest to serve and assist Him as a royal priesthood.

First Peter 2:9 says, "But you are a chosen generation, a royal priesthood, a holy nation, His own special people, that you may proclaim the praises of Him who called you out of darkness into His marvelous light." First Peter 2:5 says, "you also as living stones are being built up a spiritual house, a holy priesthood, to offer up spiritual sacrifices acceptable to God through Jesus Christ." The new and living way goes beyond the physical, enabling our spiritual sacrifices to be acceptable to God. One of the jobs of a priest is to offer sacrifices.

The church is a "spiritual house" comprised of physical people. We are the house in which God dwells. In John 17:26 Jesus said, "And I have declared to them Your name, and will declare it, that the love with which You loved Me may be in them, and I in them." Hebrews 13:16 says, "but to do good and to share forget not for with such sacrifices God is well pleased." It pleases God when we share. Sharing is a spiritual sacrifice as a result of the love from the gift of the Holy Spirit within us. When we serve God in the newness of the spirit of love, we share and freely give. The tithing of crops according to the law was administered under the Levitical priesthood. Freely giving or sharing is the administration of the new covenant (2 Cor. 9:12–13).

5

THE LAW

When Romans 7:14 says "the law is spiritual," it is not talking about the whole letter of the old covenant, which involved a physical temple, a physical priesthood, a physical inheritance, physical sacrifices, and fleshly ordinances. The law that is spiritual and reflects God's character is the law of liberty and righteousness and love as defined by the Ten Commandments. The righteousness requirements of the law apply to the new covenant (Rom. 8:4, Matt. 19:17). Jesus expounded on the spiritual administration of the law in the Sermon on the Mount. Obedience from the heart requires God's Spirit, which is given to the spiritual house or temple of God. First Peter 1:22 reveals that we obey the truth through the Spirit. This is why "no one can say that Jesus is Lord except by the Holy Spirit" (1 Cor. 12:13). Our Lord is the one we obey.

Galatians 5:18 says, "But if you are led by the Spirit, you are not under the law." We are not under the old covenant with all its additional requirements or ordinances that were imposed on physical Israel. The works of the law did not produce salvation or justification. Galatians 2:16 says, "knowing that a man is not justified by the works of the law but by faith in Jesus Christ, even we have believed in Christ Jesus, that we might be justified by faith in Christ and not by the works of the law; for by works of the law no flesh shall be justified." Through Christ we have been washed and expiated to serve "the living God." Romans 8:2 says, "For the law of the Spirit of life in Christ Jesus has made me free from the law of sin and death." The law of the Spirit is the law of love. Romans 13:11 says, "Love is the fulfillment of the law." The law of sin and death is the letter of the law that kills, but the Spirit gives life. God gives us His eternal Spirit as a guarantee of our eternal inheritance (2 Cor. 1:22). Galatians 5:16 says, "I say then: Walk in the Spirit and you shall not fulfill the lust of the flesh." When we walk in the Spirit, we walk according to the Word (Rom. 8:4). Galatians 5:19–21 mentions the works of the flesh and that "Those who practice such things will not inherit the kingdom of God." Romans 5:5 says, "The love of God is shed abroad in our hearts by the Holy Spirit which is given unto us." The Holy Spirit is given to us as a gift of love. Love involves sharing and alms giving, which we are admonished to freely do under the new covenant. In Luke 11:41 Jesus said, "but rather give alms of such things as you have." Romans 8:3–4 says, "God sending His own Son in the likeness of sinful flesh, and for sin, condemned sin in the flesh that the righteous requirements of the law might be fulfilled in us who do not walk according to the flesh but according to the Spirit."

The Spirit leads us to follow righteousness. Psalm 119:72 says, "for all Your commandments are righteousness." First John 3:10 says, "In this the children of God and the children of the devil are manifest; Whoever does not practice righteousness is not of God, nor is he who does not love his brother." Jesus is the Branch of righteousness that produces the fruit of righteousness (Jer. 23:5, Zech. 6:12). The branch also symbolized shelter. The booths Israel made from branches (Lev. 23:40–43) depict the shelter or protection we have under Christ (Isa. 4:2–6).

The law of liberty was revealed to Israel in Exodus 20. After God spoke the Ten Commandments to Israel, God spoke to Moses, the mediator of the old covenant, to speak to Israel. God through Moses added civil laws, statutes, judgments, physical sacrifices, carnal ordinances, a physical priesthood and sanctuary. Galatians 3:19 reveals that "the law was added because of transgression (the breaking of the law of liberty) till the Seed (Jesus) should come." The word *till* implies that this law of the old covenant was not to be permanent. Hebrews 8:13 and Hebrews 10:9 also confirm that the old covenant is temporary and "becoming obsolete," but the new covenant is eternal.

A Marriage Covenant

The old covenant was a type of marriage covenant binding until death (Jer. 3:14, Isa. 54:5). The death of Jesus liberated Israel from the old covenant. The old covenant was a yoke of bondage (Gal. 5:1). The old covenant was binding on Israel until death, but it could not deliver or free Israel from the bondage of sin or spiritual bondage. Hebrews 10:4 says, "The blood of bulls and of goats could not take away sins." Galatians 4:24–25 states that the earthly Jerusalem (symbolic of the old covenant) is in bondage with her children. Galatians 4:26 says, "Jerusalem above (symbolic of the new covenant) is free." As strangers and pilgrims on the earth we must press forward to the heavenly city that God has prepared for us (Heb. 11:13–16). The New Jerusalem will come down out of heaven after the first heaven and earth pass away (Rev. 21:2, 21:10).

The shed blood of Jesus also brought about a new covenant. Jesus purchased the church with His blood, so we belong to our Savior. A wife under the law was viewed as a purchased possession and a special treasure that belonged to the one who purchased her (Exod. 22:16–17). In Malachi 3:17 God talks about His future wife when it says, "They shall be Mine, says the Lord of hosts, on the day that I make My jewels," or special treasure. The marriage covenant we have with Jesus will be eternal since it is binding till death. When we are born again in the kingdom as spirit beings, we will not experience death anymore (1 Cor. 15:50–54). Revelation 21:4 says, "And God will wipe away every tear from their eyes; there shall be no more death, nor sorrow, nor crying. There shall be no more pain, for the former things have passed away."

Matthew 22:1–14 is a parable and warning for those who fail to take their invitation to the wedding seriously. We must prepare for the marriage by getting spiritually dressed. Those who fail to put on the Lord Jesus Christ (Rom. 13:14) will end up without a wedding garment. The marriage of the Lamb mentioned in Revelation 19:7–9 will occur after the resurrection when we have our celestial bodies (1 Cor. 15:40–44). Revelation 1:5 says that Jesus "loved us and washed us from our sins in His own blood." Jesus will present His bride without spot or blemish (Eph. 5:27). The called-out ones and elect are His own special people, chosen for His bride and royal priesthood (1 Pet. 2:9). The Hebrew Bible from Genesis to Malachi is divided into three divisions, the Law, the Prophets, and the Psalms, or poetic books. Luke 24:44 says, "These are the words which I spoke to you while I was still with you, that all things must be fulfilled which were written in the Law of Moses and the Prophets and the Psalms concerning Me." Although the prophecies pertaining to the physical life of Jesus and His death and resurrection have been fulfilled, many prophecies pertaining to the end-time and future reign of Jesus on earth have not yet been fulfilled.

In Matthew 5:17–18 Jesus said, "Do not think I came to destroy the law or the Prophets, I did not come to destroy but to fulfill. For assuredly, I say to you till heaven and earth pass away, one jot or one tittle will by no means pass from the law till all is fulfilled." Nothing has been changed in the law, which also contains the old covenant. Those who change the old covenant tithing laws are teaching contrary to the word of God.

Jesus has delivered us from the law so we can be married to Him. Romans 7:4 says, "Wherefore, my brethren, you also are become dead to the law by the body of Christ; that you should be married to another, even to Him who is raised from the dead, that we should bring forth fruit unto God." Ephesians 5:32 also alludes to this great mystery of a marriage between Christ and the church. The redeemed belong to Christ and are no longer under the old covenant and whole letter of the law (Deut. 27:26, Gal. 3:25, 4:5).

The law administered in the letter could only produce legalistic righteousness or self-righteousness. Philippians 3:9 says, "and be found in Him, not having my own righteousness, which is from the law, but that which is through faith in Christ, the righteousness which is from God by faith." Legalistic righteousness (Deut. 6:25) was the external righteousness of the scribes and Pharisees, which cannot get one into the kingdom of heaven. Matthew 5:20 states: "For I say to you, that unless your righteousness exceeds the righteousness of the scribes and Pharisees, you will by no means enter the kingdom of heaven." Our righteous is from God and not from the law. Second Corinthians 5:21 says, "For He made Him who knew no sin to be sin for us, that we might become the righteousness of God in Him." Second Corinthians 3:6–9 reveals that the new covenant administered in the Spirit gives life. Obedience from the heart comes by having "the mind of Christ" (1 Cor. 2:16). Without God's Spirit we cannot truly obey God since Romans 8:7 states that "the carnal (natural) mind is enmity against God; for it is not subject to the law of God, nor indeed can be." The Spirit of truth guides us into all truth (John 16:13). It is not by our own power that we obey God, but it is by the power of God in us. Second Corinthians 4:13 mentions the Spirit of faith, which is the same Spirit that Jesus has without limit. John 3:34 says, "For He whom God has sent speaks the words of God, for God does not give the Spirit by measure." Those who say that monetary tithing is commanded in the Bible are not speaking the words of God.

None of us in the flesh have reached perfection, but we are going through a purification process. First John 3:2–3 says, "Beloved, now we are children of God; and it has not yet been revealed what we shall be, but we know that when He is revealed, we shall be like Him, for we shall see Him as He is. And everyone who has this hope in Him purifies himself, just as He is pure." When God calls us, we have a choice in our conversion process. The purifying of ourselves is by the power of God. We must work out our own salvation by allowing God to work in us (Phil. 2:12–13).

The renewing of the Holy Spirit (Titus 3:5) is a day-by-day process. Second Corinthians 4:16 says, "Therefore we do not lose heart. Even though our outward man is perishing, yet the inward man is being renewed day by day." We need Jesus the Word to be our daily bread. The distress and pressures that we go through in this physical life will end up being for our benefit in the kingdom. Second Corinthians 4:17 says, "For our light affliction, which is but for a moment, is working for us a far more exceeding and eternal weigh of glory." The more we endure and overcome by the power and help of God, the more blessed we will be in the end.

Second Corinthians 3:17 says, "Now the Lord is that Spirit: and where the Spirit of the Lord is there is liberty." Jesus lives in us through the Holy Spirit. Those under the law are in bondage, and they are the children of the bondwoman (Gal. 4: 24–31). Galatians 5:18 states: "But if you are led by the Spirit you are not under the law." The law, referring to the old covenant, is the law that we are not under, and certainly the old covenant tithing laws are not for us today.

Hebrews 4:12 says, "The word of God is living and powerful." We are blessed to have the living word living in us. We must stay mindful of the things of God. The letter of the law involves ordinances of divine service with the earthly sanctuary and Levitical priesthood recorded in the first five books of the Bible. The law also contains the weightier matters of righteousness, which are to be kept under the new covenant in the Spirit.

Under the new covenant, the Holy Spirit is our teacher (John 14:26). First Corinthians 2:12–13 says, "Now we have received not the spirit of the world, but the Spirit which is from God, that we might know the things that have been freely given (without a required tithe) to us by God. These things we also speak not in words which man's wisdom teaches but which the Holy Spirit teaches, comparing spiritual things with spiritual." Second Corinthians 4:13 reveals that we have "the same Spirit of faith" that Jesus has, so we are no longer under the law or old covenant tutor.

The followers of Jesus are under the guidance of the Holy Spirit. John 14:26 also refers to the Holy Spirit as our Helper. The word Helper in Greek is also Comforter. Second Timothy 1:7 says, "For God has not given us a spirit of fear, but of power and of love and of a sound mind." God reveals spiritual knowledge to us by His Spirit. Ephesians 1:17 says, "the God of our Lord Jesus Christ, the Father of glory, may give to you the spirit of wisdom and revelation in the knowledge of Him." First John 2:27 also talks about the Holy Spirit, the spiritual anointing, unction, and endowment that teaches. The anointing of the Holy Spirit teaches us to abide in Jesus the Christ—the truth, our Potentate.

The Temple

Under the law the temple represented God's presence among Israel. Under the new covenant God's presence in not just among us, but it is in us. The indwelling of the Holy Spirit under the new covenant makes us the temple of God. First Corinthians 3:16 says, "Do you not know that you are the temple of God, and that the Spirit of God dwells in you?" Under the Law of Moses, the temple was built, supported, and maintained by the freewill offerings of the people and not by tithes (Exod. 25:1–8). Second Kings 12 shows how King Jehoash used gifts, money, and offerings to repair the temple. The money offered was used to pay carpenters and masons and stonecutters who worked on the house of the Lord. Money was also used for buying timber and hewn stone to repair the damage of the house of the Lord (2 Kings 12:11–15).

Ezra 7:16 mentions "free will offerings" freely offered to support the house or temple of God. Second Chronicles 24 talks about collecting money to repair the house of God, according to the command in Exodus 30:12–16. Offerings not tithes were designated by the Word for the support and service of the temple. The principle of giving offerings to support the temple of God is the example shown throughout both the old and new covenants. Luke 21:5 also confirms that the temple was adorned by donations, not tithes.

Second Corinthians 9:7 talks about supporting the new covenant temple of God, which is the church. Paul said to give "as he purposes in his heart." Paul used the principle mentioned in the law according to Exodus 25:2–8 to freely give offerings for the support of the temple. Paul referred to the same words of King Jehoash for supporting the temple in 2 Kings 12:4, which says, "as a man purposes in his heart."

The principle for supporting the new covenant temple, which involves the whole church, was based on the same principle used in the old covenant for supporting the physical temple. Freewill offerings are the biblical examples for supporting the temple and church of God. Second Kings 12:16 says, "the money from trespass offerings and money from the sin offerings were not brought into the house of the Lord, it belong to the priest." The agrarian tithes under the law that belong to the Levites were not a means to support the temple of God, which required maintenance.

No New Tithing Law

We should understand that we are not to take the old covenant laws on tithing and alter what has been written. To implement old covenant ordinances into the new covenant by making changes to them is not sound doctrine. Paul warns us in 2 Timothy 3:1 "that in the last days perilous times will come." It is evident to many that these stressful times are here. Second Timothy 4:3–4 states: "For the time will come when they will not endure sound doctrine, but according to their own desires, because they have itching ears, they will heap up for themselves teachers; and they will turn their ears away from the truth, and be turned aside to fables." Second Timothy 4:3–4 substantiates that among God's church there are teachers that do not teach sound doctrine. Revelation 21:4 says, "And God will wipe away every tear from their eyes; there shall be no more death, nor sorrow, nor crying. There shall be no more pain, for the former things have passed away." Sound doctrine means true, safe, uncorrupt and complete doctrine. What most churches teach on tithing is not sound doctrine.

We must realize that we must follow the instructions and example of Jesus and the apostles in the new covenant to comply with what is pertinent for the church today. Jesus told His apostles in Matthew 28:19–20: "Go therefore and make disciples of all the nations baptizing them in the name of the Father, and the Son, and of the Holy Spirit teaching them to observe all things that I have commanded you." Jesus never commanded His apostles to take tithes of any kind from His disciples.

The new covenant does not change God's law, but Romans 6:14

states: "for you are not under law but under grace." Galatians 5:18 says, "but if you are led by the Spirit, you are not under the law." The old covenant instructions for tithing and other ordinances do not apply to those who are not under the law of Moses administered under the Levitical priesthood. There are no new covenant instructions for tithing money, but false prophets may refer to the old covenant laws on tithing and change them to benefit themselves.

Under the new covenant Jesus instructed His disciples to freely give. Matthew 10:8 says, "Freely you have received, freely give." To "freely give" does not mean to enforce a payment or tithe or tax on people.

Paul made it clear that the servants of God did not preach for personal financial gain, which was a motive of false prophets (1 Tim. 6:5). In Acts 20:33 Paul said, "I have coveted no one's silver or gold or apparel. Yes you yourselves know that these hands have provided for my necessities and for those who were with me."

Paul worked to provide for himself and others with him while preaching the gospel. Some of the good news about the good news is that it was always meant to be freely given. The procedures in many churches of God is to give out free material to spread the Word. The catch is that those who join the church are coerced to pay money by being duped with a false doctrine on tithing.

Jesus Himself never requested or collected tithes from His followers while performing His ministry on earth. Jesus was supported by offerings freely given and hospitality, which is how He commanded His ministers to be supported (Mark 6:8–10; Matt. 10:7–11; Luke 9:2–4, 10:3–8). In Luke 8:1–3 when Jesus went through cities and villages preaching with the twelve apostles, various women and others provided for Him from their possessions. Mark 15:41 and Matthew 27:55 mention how some of His followers ministered to Him. The ministry of the twelve apostles never included requiring or requesting tithes from people.

The traveling ministers of Jesus who spread the gospel from one church area to another were supported by church members taking them into their homes, which meant lodging and feeding them. This is in accordance to the commands of Jesus in Matthew 10:11–14 and Luke 10:8. Second John verses 7–10 talk about "many deceivers" with false doctrines. These deceivers are not to be received—this means by taking them into your house as a place to stay, sleep, and eat (Luke 10:7) because we are not to support those who are teaching false doctrines.

Mandatory monetary tithing is a false doctrine that many support out of ignorance. To ignore what the Word of God says is ignorance, and ignorance of God's word does not bring about blessings. Some people use human reasoning when they advocate the false teaching of tithing by leaning on their own understanding or misunderstanding. Some feel that the hirelings or pastors need to be paid for their work. The Word does not mention anything about pastors being paid by taking monetary tithes. It is true that those who preach the gospel and labor for Christ have the right to receive support but not by dishonest gain. Being dishonest about what the word says about tithing to get paid is dishonest gain (Titus 1:11).

Proverbs 3:5–6 says, "Trust in the Lord with all your hearts, and lean not on your own understanding, In all your ways acknowledge Him, and He shall direct your path." When we acknowledge God, we acknowledge what His word is saying, but what most churches teach about tithing is not in accordance with God's word. We need to depend on God for support and direction. Proverbs 22:4 says, "By humility and the fear of the Lord are riches and honor and life." It is not pleasing to God when we teach, advocate, or support things contrary to His word.

6

MALACHI'S MESSAGE

Malachi 3:10 says, "Bring all the tithes into the storehouse that there may be food in My house." When Malachi talks about tithes, it is talking about food or crops with the exclusion of money. The storehouse stored crops, dried fruits, and grains. Nehemiah 10:37–38 says, "to bring the first fruits of our dough, our offerings, the fruit from all kinds of trees the new wine and oil, to the priest, to the storerooms of the house of our God; and to bring the tithes of our land to the Levites, for the Levites should receive the tithes in all our farming communities. And the priest, the descendant of Aaron, shall be with the Levites when the Levites receive tithes; and the Levites shall bring up a tenth of the tithes to the house of our God, to the rooms of the storehouse."

Nehemiah 12:44 says, "And at the same time some were appointed over the rooms of the storehouse for the offerings, the first fruits, and the tithes, to gather into them from the fields of the cities the portions specified by the Law for the priests and the Levites." Nehemiah confirms that tithes came from farming, and the law specified that these portions of crops from the field were for the Levitical priesthood.

When Malachi was written there was a famine in the land. Under the old covenant a blessing on the land with rain was a result of obedience to the law. For obedience Deuteronomy 28:8 states,

"The Lord will command the blessing on you in your storehouses and in all to which you set your hand, and He will bless you in the land which the Lord your God is giving you." Tithing crops and offering animals were carnal ordinances of the old covenant (Mal. 3:7). Israel was to observe or obey all the commandments of the Lord and His ordinances and statutes. Obedience to God brought about blessings, and Malachi addresses how Israel failed to properly obey the ordinances relating to tithes and offerings. The tithing ordinances were to be kept specifically in the way that God ordained according to His word for physical Israel.

The Levites failed to bring a tithe of the tithe of crops to the storehouse, and the priests were offering lame and sick animals on the altar (Mal. 1:7–8). The Levites and priests are the main ones that Malachi addresses for robbing God in tithes and offerings, according to Malachi 2:1 and Malachi 1:6. When Malachi 3:3 states: "He (God) will purify the sons of Levi," this will occur after the return of Jesus. Ezekiel 40:46 and 44:15 state that the Levites from the sons of Zadok will minister in the millennial temple. Malachi 3:9 and 14 confirm that even "this whole nation" failed to comply with God's ordinances according to the letter of the law.

The restoring of the kingdom of Israel will be the beginning of the restoring of the nations (Acts 1:6). Eventually there will be a restoration of all things (Acts 3:20–21), which will proceed with the return of Jesus to rule on earth for a thousand years. In the millennium there will be a physical Levitical priesthood serving in the physical temple that will be rebuilt after Christ's return (Isa. 66:20–21, Acts 15:16, Ezek. 40–45).The covenant that God made with Levi through the line of Phinehas mentioned in Numbers 25:11–13 and Malachi 2:4 will continue into the millennium. After the millennium there will be a new heaven and earth. In the New Jerusalem there will be no physical temple, so the duties of the Levitical priesthood will eventually become extinct (Rev. 21:1–2, 21:22).

The tithe of the tithe went specifically to the storehouse and was given to the sons of Aaron, who were not required to pay tithes (Num. 18:26–28). Since we are not under the Aaronic priesthood, it is evident that these tithing laws are not applicable to the new covenant. In Malachi 3:10 God says to try Him: "He will open up the windows of heaven to pour out a blessing that there will not be room enough to receive it." This verse can be taken literally when we understand that it is talking about agricultural products.

The expression "open up the windows of heaven" is an idiom which simply means that God will provide the rain to produce an abundance of crops as confirmed in Deuteronomy 28:12 and 28:8. Malachi 3:11 states that God would "rebuke the devourer." Deuteronomy 28:38 talks about the curse of locust consuming or devouring the produce. Rebuking the devourer mentioned in Malachi 3:11 would involve not allowing pests, bugs, or locusts to devour or destroy the fruit of the ground. Second Chronicles 7 revealed what God did because of Israel's sins. Second Chronicles 7:13 says, "when I shut up heaven and there is no rain, or command the locusts to devour the land, or send pestilence among My people."

Malachi 3:12 says, "And all nations will call you blessed, for you will be a delightful land, says the Lord of hosts." The blessings that God promised for tithing according to the law involved a blessing on the land with an abundance of crops to the point that Israel would not have enough room to receive the harvest into their storehouses. Deuteronomy 26:9–15 also confirms that the blessings for tithing under the law involved blessings on the land, "a land flowing with milk and honey."

Many people tithe money thinking that this will bring them an abundance of material blessings, but God's word does not promise blessings for paying monetary tithes. God's blessings on tithing are for tithing in accordance with the law and not according to the mandates of humans. Many people who never tithe are blessed with an abundance of material wealth, and many who tithe money consistently struggle financially. What God promises in His word is absolute. If our motive for paying tithes is to get, then that does not follow the flow of the Holy Spirit, which is away from self. John 7:38 says, "He who believes in Me, as the scripture has said, out of his heart will flow rivers of living water."

Malachi 4:4 says, "to remember the law of Moses." Nowhere in the law of Moses does it say that the new covenant ministers have a right to require a tithe of members' income to support them or the work of God. Nowhere in the new covenant does it state that ministers have the right to require a tithe of members' income to support them or the work of God. When we remember the law of Moses, we should remember that we are not to add on to the word that God commanded nor are we to change what is written (Deut. 4:2).

Paying monetary tithes has not been a blessing for many, but it has been an added burden placed on people by the commandments of corrupt religious leaders. Paying tithes has caused some to get in debt; it has caused added stress for some; it has caused marriage problems for some. Tithing has influenced some to leave the church because it was too difficult for them financially. Many have experienced privation while trying to pay tithes imposed on them by religious leaders abusing authority.

Single women with children making low wages have struggled to make ends meet while trying to pay tithes. College students have struggled to pay tithes when they could not afford to pay for college. Men with large families like five or more kids with low incomes have struggled to pay tithes while trying to provide for their families. Some people feel obligated to pay tithes over medical expenses, bills, and other needs because they believe the lie about monetary tithing. The longer one believes a lie, the more incredulous one may be to accept the truth.

The teaching of monetary tithing as a biblical requirement is a destructive heresy that many have been brainwashed or indoctrinated to believe. Heresies are included on the list of the works of the flesh in Galatians 5:20. Many are enticed to pay tithes by believing that they will be blessed if they do, and if they do not, they are sinning. Many who tithe are not blessed financially but are more stressed financially. A heresy is a false teaching or prevarication that does not agree or harmonize with the Word of God.

Jeremiah warns of prophets preaching lies, which seems to be on the rise in this end-time. Jeremiah 23:26 says, "How long will this be in the heart of the prophets who prophesy lies? Indeed, they are prophets of deceit of their own heart." Jeremiah 23:28 says, "And he who has My word, let him speak My word faithfully." We are not to pervert the words of the living God by making changes to what is written. Second Timothy 3:13 says, "But evil men and impostors will grow worse and worse, deceiving and being deceived." Many who are deceiving others have been deceived themselves.

Some church members can carefully budget and sacrifice to tithe while others struggle with added stress to make ends meet. This tax that has been imposed on brethren was devised to ensure gain or income for religious leaders. Many ministers are totally reliant on the tithes of members to support them and their families and their comfortable lifestyles, so no wonder why they put so much emphasis on tithing. Our emphasis should be on the truth. When we seek God, we seek the truth. Hebrews 11:6 says, "But without faith it is impossible to please Him, for he who comes to God must believe that He is, and that He is a rewarder of those who diligently seek Him." To understand the truth about tithing it has to be according to the Word.

Preachers are misleading people when they use Malachi 3:8 to try to imply you are robbing God for not paying a tithe of your monetary income to support them or the church. This agrarian tithe of the tithe mentioned in Malachi 3:10 was for the Aaronic priesthood (Num. 18:26–28). Those who try to apply the entitlement of the Aaronic priesthood upon themselves are following in the rebellion of Korah (Jude 11).

The biblical teachings on tithing do not involve a mandatory monetary tithe. The Bible has a lot to say about tithing and money, but nothing is mentioned about the tithing of money. God warns us to not add on to His word. There are examples of monetary offerings in the Bible; we also see offerings of silver, gold, and precious stones, which do not come from the seed of the land (1 Chron. 29:1–8). There are no commands or instructions for tithing silver and gold or precious stones or money anywhere in the Bible. The Bible is very explicit as to what to tithe and to whom.

7

THE DIFFERENCE IN GIVING AND PAYING

Distinguishing the difference between giving and paying is a matter of paramount importance for being blessed. The new covenant offers blessing for freely giving but not for being coerced to pay. Second Corinthians 9:7 says, "for God loves a cheerful giver." Abraham gave a tithe of the spoils because this was not required by God's law. The scribes and Pharisees paid tithes of herbs according to what was required under the law of Moses. When we understand the difference between paying tithes and freely giving then we can understand more of the freedom that we have in Christ. False prophets want to rob brethren of their freedom to freely give by mandating a tithe on church members.

Matthew 23:23 is a reference to the old covenant, which required the tithing of herbs, but the new covenant encourages giving. Under the new covenant it is a matter of freely giving instead of paying a tax or tithe that brings blessings. Jesus did not charge His disciples a fee or tithe to support Him under the new covenant. The followers of Jesus freely gave as they were able to minister to Christ and others. Luke 6:40 says, "A disciple is not above his teacher, but everyone who is perfectly trained will be like his teacher." One of the ways the apostles were like Christ their teacher was by being supported by the freely given gifts and offerings of those to whom they preached and ministered.

Jesus clearly taught giving under the new covenant. In Luke 6:38 Jesus said, "Give, and it will be given to you; good measure, pressed down, shaken together, and running over will be put into your bosom. For with the same measure that you use, it will be measured back to you." When we read Luke 6:38 we can see that Jesus did not specify a certain percent like a tithe. Luke 6:38 reveals that the amount you determine to give will determine the amount measured back to you. Paul also reiterated this in 2 Corinthians 9:6: "He who sows sparingly will also reap sparingly, and he who sows bountifully will also reap bountifully."

Giving is not limited to money. We can give of our time to serve others. We can give someone a ride if the person need transportation. We can give hospitality by having someone over for dinner. We can give encouragement, and kind words can be helpful to others. When it comes to giving to God, we can and should give thanks and praise daily. If we give others mercy, we will obtain mercy. If we give forgiveness, we can receive forgiveness. One of the reasons Paul worked as a tent maker was so that he could give as he said in Acts 20:35: "and remember the words of the Lord Jesus, that He said, 'it is more blessed to give than to receive.'"

A principle that relates to giving is in Luke 12:48, which says, "For everyone to whom much is given, from him much will be required." The implication of this verse applies to the more we know about God's will, the more we should be doing the will of God. God expects more from those who have received more. The more knowledge we have, the more talents we have, the more time we have, the more material things we have, the more we can give of these things that have been given to us from God. Ephesians 5:17 says, "Therefore do not be unwise, but understand what the will of the Lord is." God clearly reveals that His will for us under the new covenant is to freely give instead of being forced to pay a tithe.

Giving and sharing depict the love of God that has been poured out in our hearts by the Holy Spirit, which is given to us (Rom. 5:5).

Out of love God gave His Son, and Jesus gave His life as a ransom for many. A ransom means to redeem by a payment. Jesus paid it all so that we do not have to pay a penny to be saved. The Holy Spirit leads us to give and to share and to do good. James 2:15–24 reveals that our works of faith include helping the needy. Galatians 6:6 says, "Let him who is taught the word share (not tithe to) in all good things with him who teaches." One of the ways that we show love is by helping the needy (1 John 3:17).

In Philippians 4:15, Paul wrote to the saints in Philippi that "no churched shared with me concerning giving and receiving but you only." Philippians 4:16 says, "For even in Thessalonica you sent aid once and again for my necessities." Since tithing was not enforced in the early church, Paul used terns such as sharing, giving, aid, and gifts as a means by which he and others were supported. Tithing is not mentioned anywhere as a way to support the ministry or church under the new covenant. When we freely give, we glorify God. When we pay monetary tithes, we serve an incumbent of a worldly administration.

Second Corinthians 9:1 talks about "ministering to the saints." Second Corinthians 9:1–15 is not talking about a holy day offering as some try to imply, but it is talking about giving to the "needs of the saints" as 2 Corinthians 9:12 explains. Second Corinthians 9 confirms that there was no tithing system used to help the needy in the church. When 2 Corinthians 9:1 talks about "ministering to the saints," for some reason many hired preachers do not include themselves in this category because 2 Corinthians 9:7 clearly states to "give as he purposes in his heart, not grudgingly or of necessity."

Under the new covenant, no one was forced to pay a tithe to help the needy saints. Second Corinthians 9:5 reveals that under the new covenant giving is "a matter of generosity and not as a grudging obligation." When people are obligated or required to pay a tithe then that is not a matter of giving or generosity. Second Corinthians 9:11 states, "you are enriched in everything for all liberality." This liberality involves a matter of generosity in giving.

Second Corinthians 9:13 confirms that the ministry of liberal sharing is voluntary and should be done in love or out of love and to glorify God. Second Corinthians 9:13 says, "while the proof of this ministry, they glorify God for the obedience of your confession to the gospel of Christ, and for your liberal sharing with them and all men." When 2 Corinthians 9:13 mentions a liberal sharing with all men, for some reason many hired preachers do not include themselves in this category of all men. Many hired preachers do not teach to freely share with them, but they enforce paying tithes to support them. The new covenant continually expresses a liberal sharing with all men. Galatians 6:6 confirms that this liberal sharing included sharing with the ministry.

In 2 Corinthians 11:7, Paul mentioned he preached "free of charge." No tithes were required from those to whom he preached. In 1 Corinthians 9:15 we see that Paul and those associated with him also chose not to accept offerings that they had a right to receive, according to 1 Corinthians 9:15, which says, "those who serve at the altar partake of the offerings of the altar." First Corinthians 9:13 makes it clear that the new covenant ministry has the right to accept offerings for support. When it came to receiving offering, Paul said in 1 Corinthians 9:15, "But I have used none of these things." Paul did not want to abuse his authority when it came to taking offerings and material things that were freely given by brethren. Paul also felt that instead of relying on men for support, he would serve as a slave or bond servant hoping that this might win more over to Christ (1 Cor. 9:18–19).

The brethren from Macedonia supplied Paul of what he lacked, not by tithing but by sharing and giving, as Philippians 4:15 says, "no churched shared with me concerning giving and receiving but you only." Philippians 4:16 says, "For even in Thessalonica you sent aid once and again for my necessities." This aid was not a tithe but a gift or contribution to support Paul's ministry. Romans 15:25–27 talks about ministering to the poor saints in Jerusalem. Those from Macedonia and Achaia made contributions to help the poor. No tithe is mentioned as a means for helping the poor under the new covenant.

Under the new covenant, Jesus did not teach monetary tithing, but He taught the giving of alms. Luke 11:41 says, "But rather give alms of such things as you have." We should give based on what we have, and we should not give what we do not have. Alms are defined as gifts prompted by love to help the needy. The Word does not teach paying monetary tithes to support the needy, the apostles, or pastors. Cornelius the centurion, a captain of a hundred men, was referred to in Acts 10:22 "as a just man one who fears God." Cornelius being a Gentile did not pay tithes to the Levites, but he was an alms giver. Acts 10:31 states how an angel came to him and said, "your alms (charitable gifts) are remembered in the sight of God." God remembers when we give out of love, and He rewards us for our loving deeds. We honor God by helping the needy. Proverbs 14:31 says, "He who oppresses the poor reproaches his Maker, But he who honors Him (God) has mercy on the needy." Requiring money or tithes from the poor could be considered oppression. Oppression involves burdening people by the abuse of authority. When we give to the poor, then God views that as if we are giving to Him. Proverbs 19:17 says, "He who has pity on the poor lends to the Lord, and He will pay back what he has given." God blesses those who do good to others, as Matthew 25:40 states: "in as much as you did it to one of the least of these My brethren, you did it to Me." Ephesians 6:8 says, "knowing that whatever good anyone does, he will receive the same from the Lord."

God certainly wants us to help the poor and needy (Deut. 15:7). The things that are recorded in the prophets are for us to consider because what went on among physical Israel still goes on today in the church. Amos 5:12 states, "For I know your manifold transgressions and your mighty sins; Afflicting the just and taking bribes; diverting the poor from justice at the gate." Amos 5:11 states: "Therefore because you tread down the poor, And take grain taxes from him." Making the poor pay tribute or grain taxes was an example of how the house of Israel was failing to show justice to the poor. Mandating tithes from the poor is tantamount to taxing the poor, which goes on in many of the churches today.

The Word emphasizes giving to the poor instead of taking from them. God blessed Israel with an abundance of wealth starting at their exodus from Egypt to the receiving of the promised land. God's instructions for Israel for helping the poor are also mentioned in Deuteronomy 15:11: "For the poor will never cease from the land; therefore I command you, saying, "You shall open your hand wide to your brother, to your poor and your needy, in your land." To require tithes from the poor or needy is an injustice that occurs in many churches. Many church of God organizations expect tithes even form the poor no matter how poor. Blessings come when we give to the poor as Proverbs 28:27 says, "He who gives to the poor will not lack, But he who hides his eyes will have many curses." Psalm 41 reveals some of the blessings of helping the poor. Psalm 41:1–3 says, "Blessed is he who considers the poor; The Lord will deliver him in time of trouble. The Lord will preserve him and keep him alive, And he will be blessed on the earth; You will not deliver him to the will of his enemies. The Lord will strengthen him on his bed of illness; You will sustain him on his sickbed." Our God reveals throughout the scriptures His altruism for the poor, which all of us should have in Christ.

The Grace of Giving

Romans 6:14 says, "for you are not under the law but under grace." Being under grace involves having God's divine influence upon the heart. Instead of being under the law as our tutor, we now have grace to teach us. Titus 2:11–12 states: "for the grace of God that brings salvation has appeared to all men, teaching us that, denying ungodliness and worldly lusts, we should live soberly, righteously, and godly in the present age." Hebrews 10:29 and Zechariah 12:10 talk about "the Spirit of grace." God's grace grants us His power through the Spirit to worship and serve God by obeying the gospel, which includes a message of compliance (Rom. 10:16).

John 1:17 says, "For the law was given through Moses, but grace and truth came through Jesus Christ." Jesus Christ is our mediator by which we have access to the throne of grace. After God gave Israel His law of liberty, God added "the law" through Moses, the mediator of the old covenant, to speak to the children of Israel. Because we have a High Priest who is understanding and sympathetic, we can come with confidence to God's throne to obtain mercy, grace and help (Heb. 4:15–16).The reflection of grace in our lives involves receiving divine help, mercy, gifts, gratitude, unmerited favor, joy, liberality, pleasure, and forgiveness. Because of grace, "sin shall not have dominion over you" (Rom. 6:14). The more we understand grace, which includes God's divine assistance and aid, the more amazing it appears.

Second Corinthians 8:1–4 is also talking about the grace of giving. The generosity given by the churches of Macedonia of their own free will was a result of God's grace. Grace involves unmerited, undeserved favor and support freely granted. First Peter 4:10 says, "As each one has received a gift, minister it to one another, as good stewards of the manifold grace of God." The manifold grace of God involves the many forms of the grace of God. When 2 Corinthians 8:4 talks about ministering to the saints, it is not by paying tithes but by freely giving and fellowshipping or sharing by the grace of God bestowed on the churches of Macedonia.

John1:14 refers to the Word as being full of grace and truth. This grace and truth is also in the followers of Christ. John 1:16–17 says, "And of His fullness (of grace and truth) we have all received, and grace for grace." We have received grace so that we can extend grace, which involves freely giving to others. Ephesians 4:29 says, "Let no corrupt word proceed out of your mouth, but what is good for necessary edification that it may impart (minister) grace to the hearers." We do not want to teach unbiblical doctrines on tithing or anything else that fails to impart grace and truth. The grace of giving is also the giving of grace. Ephesians 2:8 says, "For by grace you have been saved, through faith and that not of yourselves, it is the gift of God." The gift of God is not something that we pay for. To enforce or require a payment or tithe from church members does not comply with the grace and liberty we have been freely given in Christ. Romans 3:24 says, "being justified freely (without any cost) by His grace, through the redemption that is in Christ Jesus."

Redemption in Christ means we have salvation by the sacrifice of Jesus our Redeemer. Romans 3:25 says, "Whom God set forth as a propitiation by His blood through faith to demonstrate His righteousness." God demonstrated His righteousness through the sinless life of Jesus, and His vicarious death was efficacious in washing away our sins. God is the justifier of the one who has faith in Jesus. Romans 1:17 says, "the just shall live by faith."

Second Corinthians 8:9 mentions the grace of Jesus: "For you know the grace of our Lord Jesus Christ, that though He was rich, yet for your sakes He became poor, that you through His poverty might become rich." Jesus being rich in righteousness became a sin offering to make us rich in righteousness. Second Corinthians 5:21 states: "For He made Him who knew no sin to be sin for us, that we might become the righteousness of God in Him." Jesus laid down all He had for us, so He became poor by giving up or laying down His life for us, according to John 15:13.

Jesus bore our iniquities, fulfilling Isaiah 53:11, and in exchange we become rich in righteousness since our righteousness is from God, according to Isaiah 54:17. Because of grace, our Lord Jesus took on our sins, and He gives us His righteousness. Paul experienced many trials, sufferings, infirmities, and maladies, but despite all that, God wanted him to know that His grace is sufficient for him (2 Cor. 12:9). By God's grace we can endure and prevail in this present evil world. Second Timothy 2:3 says, "You therefore must endure hardship as a good soldier of Jesus Christ." Second Timothy 2:1 says, "You therefore, my son, be strong in the grace that is in Christ Jesus."

Romans 4:13 says, "For the promise that he would be the heir of the world was not to Abraham or to his seed through the law, but through the righteousness of faith." Romans 5:1–2 says, "Therefore having been justified by faith we have peace with God through our Lord Jesus Christ, through whom also we have access by faith into this grace in which we stand and rejoice in hope of the glory of God." While serving the Lord we are admonished to keep rejoicing in hope, persevering in tribulation, and continuing in prayer (Rom. 12:12).

God called us through grace (2 Tim. 1:9) by the gospel "for the obtaining of the glory of our Lord Jesus Christ" (2 Thess. 2:14). Grace involves giving, and God's grace involves forgiving as Ephesians 1:7 says, "In Him we have redemption through His blood, the forgiveness of sins, according to the riches of His grace." Second Thessalonians 2:16 reveals that by grace God gives consolation and hope, which produces optimism and confidence. Titus 3:7 talks about being justified by grace while having the hope of eternal life.

With the grace that we have been given came various gifts that God wants us to use. Romans 12:6 says, "Having then gifts differing according to the grace that is given to us, let us use them." Romans 12:8 reveals that giving is one of the gifts that come from grace: "he who gives, with liberality." The giving bestowed on the churches of Macedonia in 2 Corinthians 8:1–4 is referred to as the grace of God. The gift of freely giving has been given to brethren because of God's grace. Ephesians 6:24 says, "Grace be with all those who love our Lord Jesus Christ in sincerity. Amen."

First Peter 4:10 reveals that as stewards of God's grace we should use our gift to minister to others. Many church organizations do not encourage members to use their gifts but view those not ordained as just laity, whose job is to pay, pray, stay, and do whatever the pastors say. When people fail to think for themselves, they allow others to control and rule over them. Many preachers eviscerate what the Word says on tithing to deceive and take advantage of those who trust in them to tell the truth.

Those who fail to rely on the Spirit and power of God will rely on men to tell them what to think and do. The Word tells us that we are to not put our trust in human leaders and not put our trust in man (Ps. 146:3). We can trust certain people without trusting in them. Our trust should always be in God, who is omnipotent. First Corinthians 2:5 says, "faith should not be in the wisdom of men but in the power of God."

Most ministers who rely on tithes for their own financial gain will tell you to tithe, and they may even try to convince you that it is to benefit you instead of themselves. Many people tithe because they put their trust in the pastors instead of paying attention to the Word of God. Hosea 10:13 says, "You have eaten the fruit of lies, because you trusted in your own way, in the multitude of your mighty men." Instead of trusting in the multitude, or in men, we must trust in God. God keeps us in perfect peace when we keep our minds stayed on God and trust in Him (Isa. 26:3). If we follow pastors instead of the Word, we may end up lost. Jeremiah 50:6 says, "My people have been lost sheep. Their shepherds have led them astray." We need to wake up to what is going on by many coming in the name of the Lord (Matt. 24:5).

Second Corinthians 8:12 reveals that the grace of giving is not only voluntary but "is accepted according to what one has and not according to what he does not have." We should not give what we do not have or be required to give what we cannot afford. No one should have to give grudgingly or out of compulsion. Second Corinthians 9:13 reiterates that giving under the new covenant involves a liberal sharing with all men. Galatians 5:13 says, "For you brethren have been called to liberty." Second Corinthians 9:14 says, "Thanks be to God for His indescribable gift." The gift of grace, eternal life, liberty, and love is described as indescribable.

Enforcing monetary tithes contradicts the liberty we have to freely give and "through love serve one another" (Gal. 5:13). We need grace to properly serve God. Hebrews 12:28 says, "let us have grace by which we may serve God acceptably with reverence and godly fear." Hebrews 13:9 says, "For it is good that the heart be established by grace, not with foods which have not profited those who have been occupied with them." By God's grace and kindness our hearts are strengthened, nourished spiritually, and blessed.

Second Corinthians 9:6 says, "He who sows sparingly will also reap sparingly, and he who sows bountifully will also reap bountifully." This confirms that under the new covenant it is not a matter of paying tithes to be blessed; freely giving out of generosity and love and grace with cheerfulness brings blessings. In 2 Corinthians 9:6 Paul expounds on what Jesus taught in Luke 6:38. The measure that you use or sow will be measured back or reaped. If the early new covenant church had taught to just pay a tithe and be abundantly blessed, then there would be no need for Paul to make this comment about sowing sparingly or bountifully.

Second Corinthians 9:7 says, "God loves a cheerful giver." When you freely, give as you purpose or choose, then "God is able to make all grace abound toward you, that you always having all sufficiency in all things, may have an abundance for every good work" (2 Cor. 9:8). Instead of paying money to the preachers that are well-off, we can give to the poor, and be blessed. There are many blessings mentioned throughout the Bible that come when we honor God by helping the poor.

Proverbs 22:9 says, "He who has a generous eye will be blessed, for he gives his bread to the poor." When we give then God provides so that we can give more and do good works. It is more blessed to give than to receive because when we freely give out of love, we receive more blessings from God. When we give, it is given back to us by God (Luke 6:38). When we serve God in the newness of the spirit, we freely give instead of paying a mandatory 10 percent.

First Corinthians 16:1 talks about the collection for the saints, this was as offering for the needy saints in the famine-stricken city of Jerusalem (Acts 11:28–29). Acts 11:29 states how the disciples gave according to their ability. First Corinthians 16:3 also confirms that helping the needy came from gifts and freely giving but not from tithes under the new covenant. Romans 15:26 is also talking about making contributions for the poor saints. Contributions were voluntary, made by sharing but not by mandating tithes. Ministering to the saints was a fellowship, which means a matter of sharing and freely giving. Second Corinthians 8:4 mentions "the fellowship of ministering to the saints." First Corinthians 1:9 says, "God is faithful, by whom you were called into the fellowship of His Son, Jesus Christ our Lord."

Some of the scriptures that reiterate how the new covenant church was a fellowship of freely giving and sharing are Acts 4:32–34, 2:45; Luke 6:38; 2 Corinthians 9:5–7, 9:13, 11:8–9, 8:2–4; 1 Corinthians 16:1, 9:18; Galatians 2:9–10, 6:6; Hebrews 13:16, 7:5; Philippians 4:15–16; Matthew 10:8; Luke 10:7–8; 1 Thessalonians

2:9; 2 Thessalonians 3:8. Many of these scriptures also reveal that the new covenant ministers were not paid or supported by tithes. There is a preponderance of evidence in the epistles and gospels that validate that there was no new or changed tithing system implemented in the early church. Ministers and the needy were clearly supported by the freely given donations, offerings, and hospitality of the brethren.

8

RIGHTS OF MINISTERS

F irst Corinthians 9 gives the rights of ministers. First Corinthians 9:13 states: "Those who serve at the altar partake of the offerings of the altar." First Corinthians 9:13 confirms that ministers have the right to receive offerings but not mandatory tithes. The altar represents offerings. After God made the initial covenant with Israel—the Ten Commandments mentioned in Exodus 34:28—Israel was to make an altar as mentioned in Exodus 20:24. Making an altar symbolized that the initial covenant God made with Israel was to involve a fellowship with God. Agrarian tithes were a part of the law that was added after Israel came under the Levitical priesthood. There is nothing in 1 Corinthians 9 or anywhere else in the scriptures that imply that ministers who are non-Levites have the right to require tithes of any kind.

The scripture from the law that Paul used in 1 Corinthians 9:9 to confirm that ministers under the new covenant have the right to receive support is from Deuteronomy 25:4. This verse has nothing to do with tithing. First Corinthians 9:9 says, "For it is written in the law of Moses, "you shall not muzzle an ox while it treads out the grain." There are no references to tithing under the new covenant as a means by which ministers under the new covenant are to be supported. It would be preposterous to conclude that ministers are entitled to tithes based on 1 Corinthians 9:9. First Timothy 5:18 also uses Deuteronomy 25:4 to confirm from the scriptures that elders and laborers have a right to receive support.

In 1 Corinthians 9:14 Paul referred to the instructions of Jesus, "That those who preach the gospel should live from the gospel." We have Christ's example, which involved receiving freely given offerings from His followers (Luke 8:3). The instructions of Jesus for those who preached asserted accepting hospitality and freely given support (Luke 10:7–8, Matt. 10:8–11, Mark 6:8–10).The emissary of Christ's disciples always involved freely giving to those being ministered to and freely giving from the recipients of the ministry. Matthew 10:8 says, "freely you have received, freely give." Mandating a monetary tithe is contrary to freely giving. Jesus did not command His disciples to enforce a payment or tithe or tax on those to whom they preached or ministered.

First Corinthians 9:4–7 and 1 Timothy 6:8 confirm that ministers have the right to receive support. This support involved having their needs supplied, which included food, drink, and clothing. Paul mentioned in 1 Corinthians 9:12, "Nevertheless we have not used this right, but endure all things lest we hinder the gospel of Christ." It is evident that Paul is not talking about mandatory tithing, which would have meant that the ministry would have been required to take if it was mandatory.

In 1 Corinthians 9:12 Paul used the word "we," so it was not only Paul but those associated with him that also chose not to take offerings that they had a right to receive. Paul was addressing offerings freely given by the recipients of their ministry. Paul did not want to hinder the gospel or discredit the ministry by preaching for his own personal profit. Paul expounded on how false preachers sought money and material gain, and the true ministers did not want to be associated with these wolves.

Many ministers have taken advantage of brethren and have accumulated wealth from extortion and peddling the Word (Matt. 23:25, 2 Cor. 2:17). Some people can discern and see the exploitation of corrupt teachers, which discourages some from joining a church.

Some can see how those who seem to talk the most about giving are those who are receiving the most from the giving.

Ministers associated with Paul worked so that there would be no expense or burden placed on the brethren, as 1 Thessalonians 2:9, 2 Thessalonians 3:8, and other scriptures confirm. Jesus certainly did not revise the old covenant Leviticus tithing system and implement it into the new covenant, which is what many of the churches of God do.

In Matthew 24:4 Jesus said, "Take heed that no one deceives you." This means to pay attention to God's word. We are not to change or alter what is written in the scriptures. Matthew 24:5 says, "For many will come in my name, saying, I am the Christ, and will deceive many." Who are the many that come in Christ's name, among God's church, acknowledging Jesus as the Christ and are deceiving many? Even if 90 percent of what is being preached is true, that little leaven can destroy. The more truth a false prophet preaches, the harder it may be to detect deception. A lot of truth can be proclaimed by dishonest prophets, but God sees the inner heart of those who have selfish motives or greed.

The epistle to Timothy warns us about false teachers who as 1 Timothy 6:5 states: "suppose that godliness is a means of gain." Paul was addressing elders and teachers (1 Tim. 5:17) when he wrote 1 Timothy 6:10: "For the love of money is the root of all kinds of evil, for which some have strayed from the faith in their greediness." Greed is an issue and a sin that has cause ministers to stray from the faith. Jude 3 exhorts us "to contend earnestly for the faith which was once for all delivered to the saints." The faith once delivered, according to the book of Acts, involved a fellowship of freely giving and sharing.

We are to take heed and guard our minds from deceit. Second Timothy 3:16 states: "All Scripture is given by inspiration of God, and is profitable for doctrine, for reproof, for correction, for instruction in righteousness." The doctrine of mandating monetary tithes does not come from scripture. If a doctrine does not come from scripture, then it must come from the teachings of men. What is inspired by God is not for men to change or revise.

Galatians 4:4 confirms that Jesus was born under the law, which is why He did not take the Levitical tithes for Himself since He was of the tribe of Judah. Taking the Levitical tithes while being of the tribe of Judah would have been a violation of the law. Jesus did not charge a fee or a tithe to be a part of His church that He purchased with His own blood. Mandating a tithe on brethren is equivalent to taxing brethren to be a part of an organization.

Corrupt church administrations are part of the reason why we have so many organizations of the churches of God today. Many autonomous church groups seem to be in competition with one another to get members and their money. The goal should be as Ephesians 4:13–14 states: "till we all come to the unity of the faith and of the knowledge of the Son of God, to a perfect man, to the measure of the stature of the fullness of Christ. That we should no longer be children tossed to and for and carried about with every wind of doctrine, by the trickery of men, in the cunning craftiness of deceitful plotting." Many have been tricked and connived by an unbiblical teaching on tithing.

The Jehovah's Witnesses are not correct in all their doctrines, but they are an example of an organization that applies some of the principles of the new covenant governance. The Jehovah's Witnesses do not require tithes from members; neither do they pay people to preach. The members volunteer and freely give and share their faith with others. Jehovah's Witnesses do not have a problem with splits or divisions among themselves. Financially they can accomplish much through the volunteering of members and the freely given offerings or contributions to support their growing organization.

Many people do not realize that in the history of the church of God there have been some pastors who have taught the truth on tithing by telling members that monetary tithing is not a requirement under the new covenant. These pastors have been either put out of the church, or they resigned instead of being involved in teaching a lie. Many people do not realize that out of the estimated five hundred or so groups or denominations of the churches of God (many of which came out of the worldwide organization), a few follow the new covenant example of freely giving without requiring monetary tithes.

Almost all the churches claim to be nonprofit organizations so they themselves do not have to pay taxes to the government. Many of the churches of God give out free booklets and magazines and some have websites to listen to sermons. What they claim to be free is not exactly free for the brethren. Most of the churches of God expect members to pay tithes so that they can provide this material for the public.

The early church did not pass out booklets or magazines, nor did they have computers and the technology we have today. During the time of Acts through the book of Revelation there were no expenses forced on brethren by God's ministers for preaching the gospel. Many church leaders falsely claim that monetary tithing is a biblical requirement. When a church member fails to tithe, he or she may be treated as an outcast for not complying with the man-made mandates of a pharisaical administration.

The book of Acts talks about the persecution and scattering of the church. Acts 8:4 says, "Therefore those who were scattered went everywhere preaching the word." The apostles remained in Jerusalem at that time, and scattered church members went preaching the word. Members evangelizing and sharing their faith by word of mouth is biblical, is inexpensive, and is an effective way to spread the gospel. Acts 21:8 reveals that Philip was not only a deacon but also an evangelist.

In 2 Timothy 4:5 Paul told Timothy to "do the work of an evangelist." Christians do not have to be ordained by the presbytery to evangelize, but the anointing of the Spirit inspires brethren to share the gospel. John 17:20 reveals that some will believe on Jesus Christ through our message of the word. First Peter 2:9 reveals that we are God's "own special people, that you may proclaim the praises of Him who called you out of darkness into His marvelous light." Psalm 107:22 says, "Let them sacrifice the sacrifices of thanksgiving, and declare His works with rejoicing." Rejoicing includes joyful singing, music, and dancing.

First Corinthians 16:15 talks about the household of Stephanas "and that they devoted themselves to the ministry of the saints." They did not need anyone to ordain them, but they appointed themselves. Opposition comes while doing the work of the Lord. First Corinthians 16:9 says, "There are many adversaries." Matthew 11:12 says, "The kingdom of heaven suffers violence." This verse reveals that opposition comes upon those who represent God's kingdom. We must be relentless in pressing forward in doing the work of the Lord. First Corinthians 15:58 says, "Therefore my beloved brethren be steadfast, immovable, always abounding in the work of the Lord, knowing that your labor is not in vain in the Lord." The grace of God motivates us to labor for our Lord (1 Cor. 15:10). John 10:10 says, "The thief does not come except to steal, and to kill, and to destroy." Satan is the chief thief, but Satan's ministers are followers of Satan's schemes. Among God's people there are as mentioned in 2 Corinthians 11:13–15, "deceitful workers transforming themselves into apostles of Christ." These false ministers outwardly appear to be the servants of Christ and have fooled many. There are people who do the work of the Lord deceitfully. Jeremiah pronounces a curse on those who do the work of the Lord carelessly or with slackness. Jeremiah 48:10 states: "Cursed is he who does the work of the Lord deceitfully."

A deceived or deceitful ministry extorts money from brethren by telling them that they are required to pay a tithe of their income, which is used to pay their salaries. A warning especially for hirelings is in Matthew 6:24, which says, "You cannot serve God and mammon," or riches. First Timothy 6:5 reveals that godliness is not meant to be a means for gaining money. Many use religion or the gospel for their own financial gain. Corrupt ministers will capitalize on brethren who fail to prove what the Word says about tithing.

The ministry may receive offerings of money, but pure religion was not meant to be a moneymaking business by taxing the brethren. True ministers of Christ minister for Christ instead of for money, or mammon, which is what Paul expressed in many of his epistles. When Peter addressed the elders in 1 Peter 5:1–3 he said, "Shepherd the flock of God, not for dishonest gain (not for filthy lucre or money) or as being lords over the flock but by being examples to the flock."

Mathew 23:23

Matthew 23:23 says, "Woe to you scribes and Pharisees, hypocrites! For you pay tithe of mint and anise and cummin, and have neglected the weightier matters of the law: justice and mercy and faith. These you ought to have done, without leaving the others undone." There is a lot we can glean from what Jesus had to say about tithing. Matthew 23:23, like Luke 11:42, mentions how the Pharisees tithe in accordance with the letter of the law by tithing every type of herb such as mint, anise, and cummin produced from the seed of the ground. Matthew 23 does not mention the tithing of money, which would have been an anomaly to the Jews who knew the law. The tithing of money could be categorized as unorthodox since monetary tithing is not scriptural. In Matthew 23:23 Jesus said, "these you ought to have done." Jesus was advocating agrarian tithes in accordance with the law that the Jews were under at that time. To teach tithing different from the law such as mandatory monetary tithing is simply contrary to the Word of God.

One thing Matthew 23:23 makes clear is that tithing does not put you in a good relationship with God as some false prophets may imply. We see how the Pharisees diligently tithed in accordance with the law, and Jesus referred to them as hypocrites, fools, and blind, which is not how I would describe someone who has a good relationship with God. Communicating through prayer and listening to the Word are integral deeds for a good relationship with God. Sadly, many fail to listen to what the Word says about tithing, but many will believe the lies that men teach on this subject.

Matthew 23:23 reveals that tithing is *not* one of the weightier matters of the law. The hypocrites tithed but neglected the weightier matters of the law such as justice, mercy, and faith. A person can tithe according to the law and still not have faith. First Corinthians 13:3

reveals how one can give all he has to feed the poor, but if he does not have love, it profits him nothing. Luke 11:42 reveals that one can tithe and pass by or ignore justice and the love of God. The Pharisees put more emphasis on the physical instead of the spiritual matters of the law, which are the weightier matters or more important things. Tithing was a physical, carnal ordinance of the old covenant imposed on those under the Levitical priesthood. God's love is spiritual, and it is love that God wants us to have and give to others.

When we serve God in the newness of the spirit we are delivered from the carnal ordinances of the old covenant. Through the Spirit we keep the weightier matters of the law, which are included in both the old and new covenants. We do not keep the whole letter of the law with all its physical requirements, as explained in the book of Hebrews. The epistles of Paul expound on the reformation and many changes from the old to the new covenant. We cannot change the old covenant or revise its ordinances. We are blessed to be under a new and better covenant without all the added physical and temple ordinances.

Jesus introduced a new covenant, which involves a new and living way (Heb. 10:20). The reformation brought about a new priesthood with Jesus as our High Priest (Heb. 8:1). With the new covenant we have a new sanctuary not set up by men (Heb. 8:2). The new covenant involves a new and living sacrifice with Christ living in us (Rom. 12:1). With the new covenant we have a more excellent ministry with Jesus as our Mediator (Heb. 8:6). With the new covenant we become a new creation (2 Cor. 5:17). We have a new commandment to love as Christ loves (John 13:35). It is only by the power of the Spirit given to the church that we can keep this commandment (Rom. 5:5).

Rightly Dividing the Word

Paul told Timothy in 2 Timothy 2:15, "Be diligent (study) to present yourself approved to God, a worker who does not need to be ashamed, rightly dividing the word of truth." When we rightly divide the word of truth we divide or separate the old from the new, the letter from the spirit, the weightier matters from the not so weightier matters, the physical from the spiritual, the transitory from the eternal, the prophecy from the history, the passing from the permanent, and the children of the flesh from the children of the promise.

The promises of spiritual blessings were to Abraham and his Seed, being Jesus (Gal. 3:16). Galatians 3:29 says, "And if you are Christ's then you are Abraham's seed, and heirs according to the promise." Genesis 22:18 and Genesis 12:3 say, "And in you all the families of the earth shall be blessed." The Seed Jesus came from the lineage of Abraham. This blessing involves salvation and receiving the Holy Spirit. Galatians 3:14 states: "that the blessing of Abraham might come upon the Gentiles in Christ Jesus, that we might receive the promise of the Spirit through faith." First Peter 1:23 reveals that Jesus is the incorruptible Seed through the word of God. Jesus is the Seed that was prophesied to prevail over Satan the serpent (Gen. 3:15). Jesus is the Seed that produces the blessed life.

To rightly divide the Word also means to cut into or dissect and analyze the Word. We should be thorough and meticulous, and search for the truth. We need to be precise, exact, or accurate in interpreting to Word by the Word. Our hermeneutics should involve considering all the facts. Isaiah 28:9 reveals that we need to go beyond the milk of the Word to get more understanding and knowledge. Relating to Matthew 23:24, it is good to "strain out a gnat," or pay attention to the little things as long as we do not "swallow a camel" or ignore the big things. If we pay attention and examine what God's word says concerning tithing, it will be clear that what most churches teach on this subject does not concur with the Word.

Working Ministers

Why did Paul, Silvanus, Timothy, Barnabas, Titus, and other prominent ministers associated with Paul choose to work to support themselves while preaching the gospel? First Thessalonians 2:9 confirms that the ministers of the gospel worked so that they might not be a burden to others by relying on financial aid. Second Thessalonians 3:8–10 states that they worked to not be a burden to others, and as ministers they wanted to be an example to the brethren.

Second Thessalonians 3:8 says, "nor did we eat anyone's bread free of charge, but worked with labor and toil night and day, that we might not be a burden to any of you." The church of God at Thessalonica had members who were not working but relied on the handouts and generosity of brethren for food. As a result of this, Paul mentioned that as ministers they would set the example and work. Paul declared in 2 Thessalonians 3:10 that "if anyone will not work, neither shall he eat."

In Acts 20:35 Paul says, "I have shown you in every way, by laboring like this, that you must support the weak." Acts 18:3 explains how Paul labored as a tentmaker to supply for his own needs and for those with him. Titus was a Gentile convert from Antioch who was one of the ministers working with Paul. Working to support the weak was one of the good works that Titus, Paul, and other ministers did to be an example to others. First Corinthians 9:18–19 reveals that Paul worked because he did not want to take advantage of others. In 1 Corinthians 10:33 Paul mentioned that he was not seeking his own profit, but he wanted others to profit "that they may be saved." Maybe more ministers should be imitators of Paul as he imitated Christ (1 Cor. 11:1). In 1 Corinthians 9:18 Paul said that he wanted to "present the gospel of Christ without charge." The words "without charge" in the Greek means without any expense to others. This would include without enforcing tithes on anyone. In 1 Corinthians 9:19 Paul claimed to be "free from all men." Paul did not want to be dependent on others for support. In 2 Corinthians 11:7, Paul again mentioned that he preached "free of charge" or without requiring financial aid. In 2 Corinthians 11:8–9, even when Paul was in need, he could still claim that he was not a burden to those he preached to. Paul said that he "robbed other churches taking wages" (not tithes) to minister to the Corinthians. The word *robbed* in verse 8 does not mean that Paul was stealing, but it means that he deprived them of what they had a right to have. The word *wages* in verse 8 means "rations for a soldier," which is not a reference to tithes. The brethren from Macedonia supplied Paul of what he lacked by freely giving and sharing, as Philippians 4:15 confirms.

Paul said in 2 Corinthians 11:12, "But what I do, I will also continue to do." Paul was talking about preaching the gospel free of charge (2 Cor. 11:7, 1 Cor. 9:18). Paul chose not to accept financial support to cut off the opportunity of false apostles who wanted to boast that they were apostles just like him and his associates. The false apostles were deceitful workers preaching for financial gain (2 Cor. 11:13) and even peddling the word. In 2 Corinthians 2:17 Paul said, "For we are not as so MANY peddling the word of God." Peddling means selling or making people pay to hear the word. False prophets may preach the word for money or other wrong motives. Enforcing monetary tithes on brethren is a way of peddling the word of God.

The word *peddling* in 2 Corinthians 2:17 in the Greek means "adulterating for gain." Second Peter 2:14 talks about false teachers "having eyes full of adultery." Jeremiah 23:14 says, "Also I have seen a horrible thing in the prophets of Jerusalem: They commit adultery and walk in lies." Although Balaam preached the truth, he prostituted his prophetic gift for pay. Second Peter 2:15 talks about those among God's church, following the way of Balaam, who have been "trained in covetous practices" and "who love the wages of unrighteousness."

Many ministers in the churches of God were taught by the man who started the worldwide church of God and were indoctrinated with the doctrine of the Nicolaitans. Many ministers were trained in following the way of Balaam, which involved preaching for pay. The bureaucracy set up in the organization influenced some to pursue status. Men coveted preeminence, money, titles, and positions paying higher salaries and authority that they abused.

What went on with old covenant Israel stills goes on today among spiritual Israel. The true prophets warn us about the corruption of the leaders among God's people. Jeremiah 6:13 is reiterated in Jeremiah 8:10, which says, "Because from the least of them even to the greatest of them, Everyone is given to covetousness; And from the prophet even to the priest, Everyone deals falsely." God's church is referred to as His house, and in Jeremiah 23:11 God says, "For both prophet and priest or (chief ruler) are profane; Yes, in My house I have found their wickedness."

Jeremiah 23:1 says, "Woe to the shepherds who destroy and scatter the sheep of My pasture! says the Lord." God does not charge a fee to eat from His pasture (Isa. 55:1–3, Deut. 23:24–25, Matt. 10:8). The result of the way of Balaam and the deeds of the Nicolaitans within the church has produced many divisions. Paul talks about the church as a body. First Corinthians 12:24–25 says, "But God composed the body, having given greater honor to that part which lacks it, that there should be no schism (division) in the body, but that the members should have the same care for one another."

Ephesians 4:16 talks about the whole body working effectively when "every part does its share." All of us have a part to play in causing the "growth of the body for the edifying of itself in love." First Corinthians 12:12–29 talks about the body being one with many members. Different parts of the body have different functions, but all the members are connected to the same head. Ephesians 5:23–24 affirms that the head of the church is the Savior of the body, to whom we are to be subject to in everything. Jesus said in Matthew 23:8 that we are all brethren. Those who put themselves above others in the body do not receive greater honor from God, which is why "many who are first will be last, and the last first" (Matt. 19:30). First Corinthians 12:4–11 talks about various gifts and diversities of activities. First Corinthians 12:7 says, "But the manifestation of the Spirit is given to each one for the profit of all." God wants the whole body to profit from the gifts He gives. Certain responsibilities in the church like that of a bishop or overseer pertain to men (1 Tim. 3:1–2) but women are not excluded from serving with the gifts that they have from God. Philippians 4:3 mentions women that labored in the gospel. Romans 16:3 mentions women being fellow workers in Christ Jesus.

Romans 16:1 mentions Phoebe, a sister and servant of the church in Cenchrea. This word *servant* in Greek is deaconess. The Bible mentions women prophetesses such as Anna, Miriam, and Deborah (Luke 2:36, Exod. 15:20, Judg. 4:4, Acts 21:9). Acts 2:17 says, "Your sons and daughters shall prophesy" as a result of the pouring out of the Spirit. Acts 2:18 includes maidservants as those who will prophesy. To prophesy involves edifying, exhorting, and comforting others (1Cor. 14:3). Women are included in the Bible in proclaiming God's truth.

The third epistle of John verse 9 addresses the lack of hospitality shown to itinerant preachers by Diotrephes who would not receive them by providing for their needs. The practice taught by Jesus was to lodge and feed those who labored in preaching the gospel. Diotrephes even went as far as putting brethren out of the church who wished to take in those laboring for Christ. Third John 9 mentions how Diotrephes loved to have preeminence among the church. Diotrephesism is still a problem in the church today.

Some ministers want to have preeminence and control and even discourage others in laboring for the Word. Third John 7 mentions that those who journeyed took nothing from the Gentiles. They were not out to get money like many of the false preachers. John encouraged the church to receive ministers in their homes by lodging and feeding them, which reiterates that the support of the ministry was through hospitality and the giving of offerings.

Paul described the life of the apostles and ministry in his day as being like a poorly treated slave. First Corinthians 4:11–13 states, "To the present hour we both hunger and thirst, and we are poorly clothed, and beaten and homeless. And we labor, working with our own hands (the ministry worked—had jobs like common people) Being reviled we bless; being persecuted we endure; being defamed, we entreat. We have been made as the filth of the world, the off scouring of all things until now."

The standard of living for many preachers today is drastically different from what Paul experienced. In 2 Corinthians 6:3–10 Paul talks about their ministry living in a way to not give offense in anything, "that the ministry may not be blamed," or to be without fault. Paul describes the ministers in 2 Corinthians 6:10 as poor and as having nothing. The lifestyle of the early church ministry was not so luxurious.

In 2 Corinthians 11:23–28 Paul compares his lifestyle to that of false ministers. Instead of living in comfort at the expense of taking tithes from brethren, Paul experienced toil or hard work, persecution, privation, perils, and poverty while preaching and ministering to others. The modest lifestyle of serving as a slave and even suffering was what Paul used to authenticate the ministry of Christ. Paul declined his right to accept material things to validate the fact that he was not associated with the many deceitful workers. Paul mentioned in 1 Corinthians 9:18 that he did not want to abuse his authority in the gospel, which was a characteristic of false prophets.

The Bible mentions some of the occupations of the early new covenant ministers. Peter, Andrew, James, John, Thomas, and other disciples were fishermen and went back to fishing even after the death of Jesus (John 21:3). In Paul's letter to Titus he requested that Titus send Zenan, a minister who was also a lawyer (Titus 3:13). Paul still referred to Luke as "the beloved physician" in Colossians 4:14, written about thirty years after the death of Jesus. Matthew was a tax collector (Matt. 10:3). We know even Paul worked as a tentmaker while preaching the gospel (Acts 18:3). There are numerous references to ministers working to support themselves to not be a financial burden on others. There are no examples in the new covenant of ministers being paid by taking tithes from church members.

9

SCRIBES AND PHARISEES

J esus expressed His disapproval toward the scribes and Pharisees while He was on earth, and we need to see how what Jesus said applies today. Just who are the modern-day scribes and Pharisees? The scribes and Pharisees were a reference to the "blind guides," according to Matthew 23:16 and 24. When Jesus was addressing the scribes and Pharisees, He was talking about blind religious leaders, who are still among us today. In Matthew 15:14 when Jesus referred to the Pharisees He said, "They are blind leaders of the blind. And if the blind leads the blind, both will fall into a ditch." If we are led by blind leaders instead of being led by God's Spirit, we will also fall into a ditch. A dangerous thing about being spiritually blind is that people who are spiritually blind fail to see that they are blind.

The scribes and Pharisees were appointed by the Romans to be the religious leaders among the Jewish people. The scribes and Pharisees sat in Moses's seat, according to Matthew 23:1. Those who sat in Moses's seat judged matters over the people according to the law of Moses. These religious leaders made judicial decisions based on God's statutes and laws (Exod. 18:14–16). The scribes and Pharisees were the Sanhedrin, the high court over the Jewish people. The scribes and Pharisees were considered highly educated in the word of God, but they also believed in the Mishnah or oral law with its traditions. These traditions included things that were not according to the word of God (Mark 7:5–13). Enforcing monetary tithing has become a tradition in the church that is not according to the Word. We are told in Luke 12:1 to "beware of the leaven of the Pharisees, which is hypocrisy." Matthew 16:11–12 also talks about the leaven of Pharisees, which involves doctrines or teachings that do not come from the word of God. Jesus was addressing the scribes and Pharisees, the hypocritical religious leaders, in Matthew 15:8–9, which says, "This people draws near unto me with their mouth, and honors me with their lips; but their heart is far from me. And in vain they worship Me, teaching as doctrines the commandments of men." When men add on to God's law or teach things that are not according to the Word, then they are the commandments of men, and we need to be aware of this leaven.

First Corinthians 5:8 reveals that God's word is "the unleavened bread of sincerity and truth." When men add on to the word of God, they are adding leaven to what God proclaimed as unleavened. Many are making the mistake of Nadab and Abihu by adding something that was not commanded by God. Leviticus 10:1 says, "Then Nadab and Abihu, the sons of Aaron, each took his censer and put fire in it, put incense on it, and offered profane fire before the Lord, which He had not commanded them." Monetary tithing was added by men, but it is not something that is commanded by the Word.

We should learn from the mistake of Aaron's sons, who failed to comply with what God commanded. God gave explicit instruction on tithing for the old covenant, and we cannot circumvent what is written in the Word. When men add to or change what God commands, then that can involve imposing burdens on people. One of the attributes of blind leaders included binding heavy burdens on people, according to Matthew 23:4.

Many of the churches of God expect members to pay 20 percent, or two tithes of their monetary income, every third year out of seven. Along with these tithes, members are expected to save another tithe for the annual feast along with giving offerings. Paying various tithes has been difficult or onerous for many in the church. Members making minimum wage or living paycheck to paycheck are often stressed and burdened by paying an additional tithe from their low incomes.

Even members with high incomes have been oppressed while trying to pay this added tithe commanded by men. Added regulations by men are often burdens implemented by leaders abusing authority. The heavy yoke and burden mentioned in 1 Kings 12:4 under the old covenant involved excessive taxes by Solomon. One of the ways Jesus made His yoke easy—the yoke of the new covenant—was by allowing people to freely give based on ability and choice (Matt. 11:29–30, 10:8; 2 Cor. 9:7, 8:12; Luke 6:38).

Acts 15:5–11 addresses one of the conflicts in the early church relating to Gentile believers. Some Pharisees taught adherence to the law of Moses, which meant keeping the old covenant. Acts 15:5 says, "But some of the sect of the Pharisees, who believed rose up, saying, "It is necessary to circumcise them, and to command them to keep the law of Moses." Peter was inspired to resolve this by saying in Acts 15:8, "So God, who knows the heart, acknowledged them by giving them the Holy Spirit, just as He did to us, and made no distinction between us and them, purifying their hearts by faith." In Acts 15:10 Peter accused the Pharisees of "putting a yoke on the neck of these disciples." Peter was talking about the yoke of the old covenant. Jesus loosed us from the yoke of the letter of law with all its legalistic ordinances. Through the Holy Spirit we now worship God in the Spirit of truth.

Another attribute of the blind religious guides mentioned in Matthew 23:25 revealed that they were "full of extortion." Extortion means to obtain by force, intimidation, cunning deception, and abuse of authority. An extortionist is one who is involved in cheating others. Telling people that they are required to pay monetary tithes by altering the scriptures is a lie, cunning deception, and extortion. Corrupt leadership involves incorrect teachings by changing God's law, and no one has the authority to change God's Word. Those who cannot see the clear changes that men have made to the tithing laws may need to have their eyes anointed so that they may see.

In Luke 16:13–14 Jesus said, "No servant minister can serve two masters; You cannot serve God and mammon." Luke 16:14 states: "Now the Pharisees who were lovers of money, also heard all these things and were scoffing Him." In Luke 16:15 Jesus was addressing the Pharisaic religious leaders and said, "For what is highly esteemed among men is an abomination in the sight of God." This can apply to things and people. In Luke 6:26 Jesus said, "Woe to you when all men speak well of you, for so did their fathers to the false prophets." Jesus described the scribes and Pharisees in Matthew 23:28 as, "Even so you also outwardly appear righteous to men, but inside you are full of hypocrisy and lawlessness."

The Word reveals that the false prophets are often praised by men and that the true prophets are often persecuted. Jesus said in Matthew 5:11–12: "Blessed are you when they revile and persecute you, and say all kinds of evil against you falsely for My sake. Rejoice and be exceedingly glad, for great is your reward in heaven, for so they persecuted the prophets who were before you." The history of the people of God reveals that they often admired false prophets instead of the true prophets of God. Second Chronicles 36:16 records, "But they mocked the messengers of God, despised His words, and scoffed at His prophets, until the wrath of the Lord arose against His people, till there was no remedy."

The ones that had the biggest problem with Christ when he was on earth were the religious leaders who He rebuked. Things have not changed, since the same things are going on today with corrupt leadership among God's people. Many still put false ministers who appear so righteous on a pedestal and praise them, and yet many are involved in abusing authority, extortion, and dishonest gain. Some may be doing these things out of ignorance or a lack of understanding, but for those ministers who know that monetary tithing is not scriptural and are still imposing it on brethren, I would say, woe to them. First Corinthians 6:10 includes extortionists as those who will not inherit the kingdom of God.

10

THE TRUE TREASURE

One of the cunning lines used by some preachers to get money is by quoting Luke 12:34, which states: "For where your treasure is there your heart will be also." But to understand this verse we need to consider the preceding verses that talk about two types of treasure and about giving alms or gifts prompted by love to help the needy. The two types of treasure involve the earthly treasure and the heavenly treasure. The heavenly treasure is mentioned in Luke 12:33: "a treasure in the heavens that does not fail, where no thief approaches nor moth destroys." The treasure in the heavens is not talking about money. Luke 16:9–11 refers to the worldly wealth as "unrighteous mammon." First Peter 1:18 says we were not redeemed with corruptible or perishable things like silver or gold. The "true riches" mentioned in Luke 16:11 are spiritual and eternal.

In Luke 12:15 Jesus said, "Take heed and beware of covetousness, for one's life does not consist in the abundance of things he possesses." Our focus should be predominantly on the spiritual and not the physical. Colossians 2:3 tells us to "set your mind on things above, not on things on the earth." We need to look forward to what God wants to give us, which goes beyond what we can fathom. Paul said in Ephesians 3:8, "unto me who am less than the least of all saints is this grace given, that I should preach among the Gentiles the unsearchable riches of Christ."

Trying to accumulate wealth in this life is a secular pursuit that can distract us from finding the true treasure of God. In Luke 12:21 Jesus said, "so is he who lays up treasure for himself, and is not rich toward God." The physical and spiritual treasure that God blesses us with should be shared with others to please God. Our focus should be on pleasing God in all that we do.

A point repeatedly made in the Bible is that our true treasure is spiritual and not physical or monetary. Luke 16:10–11 refers to the unrighteous mammon or worldly wealth as the least of all riches. God wants us to treasure the truth and understand the value of wisdom. Proverbs 3:13–15 says, "Happy is the man who finds wisdom, and the man who gains understanding; For her proceeds are better than the profits of silver, and her gain than fine gold, she is more precious than rubies, and all the things you may desire cannot compare with her."

Job 28:12–28 expounds on the value of wisdom and understanding. Gold, silver, precious gems, crystal, topaz, and rubies cannot equal the value of wisdom and understanding. Job 28:28 says, "And to man He said, Behold, the fear of the Lord, that is wisdom, and to depart from evil is understanding." Out of all the things that we may desire, wisdom and understanding should be at the top of the list. There is nothing in this physical world that is more important or valuable than God's Word. Job went through his trials and suffering, but he had the faith to persevere. Regardless of what we go through in this life, we must not give up on God. Our Savior does not leave (fail) us nor forsake us (Heb. 13:5).

The psalmist of Psalm 119 realized that having God's law was more beneficial than having money. Psalm 119:72 says, "The law of Your mouth is better to me than thousands of coins of gold and silver." Psalm 119:162 says, "I rejoice at Your word as one who finds great treasure." Colossians 2:2–3 talks about "all riches of the full assurance of understanding, to the knowledge of the mystery of God, both of the Father and of Christ, in whom are hidden all treasures of wisdom and knowledge." It is an awesome treasure to have the wisdom and knowledge of God, which comes through the Holy Spirit and the Word.

Understanding God's Word and having the wisdom of God, which is without partiality, is the true treasure. First Peter 1:7 mentions the "faith being much more precious than gold that perishes." When we treasure the truth then our hearts will also be on the truth. The treasure for many false prophets is money or mammon, which is why they devise cunning lies to get your money. Paul emphasized that deacons, bishops, and laborers for Christ were not to be greedy for money, which was a characteristic of false prophets. Paul promoted working while being involved in the ministry to set an example (2 Thess. 3:8–9). Paul made a distinction between the true servants of God and the false preachers who "teach things which they ought not, for the sake of dishonest gain" (Titus 1:11). Mandatory monetary tithing is a doctrine that is taught by many that they ought not.

Paul mentioned in 1 Timothy 6:9: "But those who desire to be rich fall into temptation and a snare, and into many foolish and harmful lusts which drown men in destruction and perdition." This verse that can apply to many people is specifically addressed to teachers and elders (1 Tim. 5:17, 6:3). First Timothy 6:5 talks about those "who suppose that godliness is a means of gain." Putting on piety and using the gospel became a scheme of false prophets for making money. When we look at the examples in the early church, we can see that ministering the gospel was not meant to be a means for accumulating personal wealth. Money had a big influence on the apostasy that started in the early church.

To be rich is not a sin, but to be rich, greedy, and selfish is sin. The rich are admonished to use their wealth to serve others. First Timothy 6:17–18 states: "Command those who are rich in this present age not to be haughty, nor to trust in uncertain riches but in the living God, who gives us richly all things to enjoy. Let them do good, that they be rich in good works, ready to give, willing to share." The theme of giving and sharing is pontificated throughout the new covenant because that is what love involves. When we serve God in the newness of the Spirit, there are no legalistic monetary tithes required. In Christ we can be poor in material things as Paul described the life of the apostles in his time in 1 Corinthians 4:11, but in Christ we can still be rich in good works, faith, and righteousness.

We must be careful to not judge others based on how much or how little they give. We do not always know people's circumstances or motives. People can give for the wrong reasons like the hypocrites "to be seen by men," as mentioned in Matthew 6:1. The poor giving a little was viewed as being more than the rich giving a lot by Christ in the case of the poor widow in Luke 21:1–4. The poor giving a dollar can be more generous than the rich giving a hundred dollars.

One person may give one hundred dollars to help the poor; someone else may give two hours of their time in fervent prayer for the poor. From God's perspective, do we know who gave the most? When we give out of love and do good deeds our Father sees and rewards us for our good works (Matt. 6:4). Ephesians 6:8 says, "whatever good anyone does, he will receive the same from the Lord." When we do good, we will receive good from God. It is important that we freely give, which means we have the freedom to whom and of how much we give.

The church of God in Corinth had major problems with false teachers, "handling the word of God deceitfully," as mentioned in 2 Corinthians 4:2. This handling of the word deceitfully literally means in the Greek adulterating the word of God. Along with tampering with God's word, many were making people pay by charging a fee for preaching the word (2 Cor. 2:17). Isaiah 55:1–3 is a message about the spiritual food, which God freely gives, and how many spend money for what is not bread. There should not be a fee for what Jesus gave to us free. Matthew 10:7–8 and John 6:27 confirm that the Word gives the food that endures to everlasting life. There is no tax or cost for what is freely given. In John 17:14 Jesus said, "I have given them Your word." Our salvation involves the gift of eternal life, which is not something we can pay for or earn on our own efforts.

One of the characteristics of false teachers in the new covenant was that they were involved in Judaizing or teaching that converts had to obey the Mosaic law. In many of the churches of God the ministers use the Mosaic law to teach monetary tithing even though the law does not teach monetary tithing. If a teaching does not match the word of God, then it is a false doctrine. Ephesians 5:6 says, "Let no one deceive you with empty words." Empty words would include words that cannot be substantiated by the word of God. Many are presumptuous about accepting a doctrine on tithing that they cannot prove by the word of God. To agree with God, our belief must be according to the Word.

The mundane and monetary treasures of men can be a stumbling block for many in accumulating the true treasures of God. Matthew 19:23 says, "Then Jesus said to His disciples, Assuredly, I say to you that it is hard for a rich man to enter the kingdom of heaven." If we are in a situation where we must give up everything to follow Christ, those who have an abundance may have a harder time giving up what they have for Christ's sake.

In Matthew 19:17–22 the young rich man had a problem separating from his great possessions to be with Christ. Sometimes with wealth we fall into temptations (1 Tim. 6:9). Matthew 13:22 mentions how the deceitfulness of riches can choke the word and cause us to become unfruitful. The worldly riches are temporary, but the riches of God's grace are eternal (Eph. 1:7, 2:8). Our security comes from Yeshua the Christ and not from physical things. Sometimes with wealth comes pride. First Peter 5:5 says, "God resists the proud, but gives grace to the humble."

People who are affluent often consume their time and efforts with the responsibilities involved in handling wealth. Many people put their worldly goods before God and make a god out of material things. Physical wealth can cause people to take their focus off the spiritual treasure. A dollar bill may say "in God we trust," but so often those who have an abundance of money put their trust in money instead of in God. A warning especially to the false teachers is 1 Timothy 6:10, which says, "the love of money is a root of all kinds of evil." This evil would include false doctrines about tithing.

Ministers need to remember what Jesus said to His apostles in Luke 22:25: "And He (Jesus) said to them, When I sent you without money bag, knapsack and sandals, did you lack anything?" So they said, "Nothing." Ministers need to trust in God and not in taking tithes from people to minister. Proverbs 28:25 states: "He who is of a proud heart stirs up strife, But he who trusts in the Lord will be prospered." Proverbs 29:25 says, "the fear of man brings a snare, but whoever trusts in the Lord shall be safe."

Second Corinthians 4:6–7 says, "For it is the God who commanded light to shine out of darkness, who has shone in our hearts to give the light of the knowledge of the glory of God in the face of Jesus Christ. But we have this treasure in earthen vessels, that the excellence of the power may be of God and not of us." Colossians 1:27 says, "Christ in you the hope of glory." God gives us a vision of the things that are spiritual. Ephesians 1:18 says, "the eyes of your understanding being enlightened; that you may know what is the hope of His calling, what are the riches of the glory of His inheritance in the saints." We need to stay focused on our fabulous future of fellowship in the glory of God. While we are terrestrial beings, we can possess the wonderful, spiritual, and true treasure of God.

Two Types of Servants

Many people fail to realize that the Bible reveals two types of servants. The two types of servants involve bond servants and hired servants. The term *bond servant* is sometimes translated as slave. The term bond servant is derived from the words *bondage* and *servant*. Bondage is a term that relates to slavery. Bond servants were not paid but had their basic needs provided for so that they could serve their masters. Hired servants were generally paid money for their work.

Leviticus 25:39 addresses the two types of servants. Bond servants were purchased possessions and became the property of the one who purchased them (Lev. 25:42–45). Israelites were the bond servants of God, so they were not to be bond servants of other Israelites (Lev. 25:42). According to the law, the Israelites who became poor and sold themselves were not compelled to serve as bond servants but as hired servants. Leviticus 25:39–40 states: "And if one of your brethren who dwells by you becomes poor, and sells himself to you, you shall not compel him to serve as a (bond servant) slave, as a hired servant and a sojourner he shall be with you, and shall serve you until the year of jubilee."

The New King James Version is one of the better translations that make the distinction between the two types of servants. Another reason why the apostles were not paid to preach is that they followed the example of Jesus of being a bond servant. Philippians 2:7 is a statement about Jesus that says, "but made Himself of no reputation, taking the form of a bondservant." First John 2:6 states: "He who says he abides in Him ought himself also to walk just as He walked." Being a bond servant of God offers true liberty. God brought Israel out of Egyptian slavery so that they could serve Him as bond servants and have freedom (Exod. 8:1, Lev. 25:42).

Philippians 1:1 starts by Paul acknowledging that he and Timothy were bond servants of Jesus Christ. The book of James starts with "James a bondservant of God and the Lord Jesus Christ." Second Peter 1:1 says, "Simon Peter a bondservant and apostle of Jesus Christ." Jude 1:1 says, "Jude a bondservant of Jesus, and brother of James." James 1:1 says, "James a bondservant of God and the Lord Jesus Christ."

Paul mentioned in Colossians 4:12: "Epaphras, who is one of you, a bondservant of Christ, greets you always laboring fervently for you in prayers, that you may stand perfect and complete in all the will of God." The disciples who wrote epistles reiterated the fact that they were bond servants, which confirmed that they were not hired servants who preached for pay. Being a bond servant was the example of Jesus Christ that His disciples followed in doing the work of God (Phil. 2:7).

When Philippians 2:5 says, "Let this mind be in you which was in Christ Jesus." This is also talking about having the attitude of a bond servant (Phil. 2:7). Mary the mother of Jesus was called the maidservant of the Lord (Luke 1:38). The word *maidservant* means bond slave. Mary revealed some important factors that made her blessed as a bond slave. Mary declared the greatness of God, acknowledged His benefits, and rejoiced in her Savior. Mary realized that God regarded her humble state of mind while being a maidservant (Luke 1:46–50). Bond servants were considered the lowest of servants. Being a hired servant was considered more prestigious than being a bond servant in human society. In Luke 6:40 Jesus said, "A disciple is not above his teacher, but everyone who is perfectly trained will be like his teacher." Jesus was a bond servant and did not require tithes of any kind but accepted the freely given contributions by His followers. In 2 Corinthians 4:5 when Paul talked about the ministry, Paul said, "For we do not preach ourselves, but Christ Jesus the Lord, and ourselves your bondservants for Jesus' sake."

Unless you understand what being a bond servant involves you will not really grasp what Paul is saying in 2 Corinthians 4:5. Paul preached and practiced what Jesus preached. For the sake of Jesus, the early church ministry served as bond servants. Bond servants were supported by having their basic needs met, which is why Paul said in 1 Timothy 6:8: "And having food and clothing with these we shall be content." Being a bond servant was a part of the ministry of the apostles, prophets, and Jesus Christ.

Revelation 2:20 mentions a church administration where God's servants are seduced by the woman Jezebel, which represents a false church. Jezebel incited Ahab the king of Samaria to sell himself to do evil (1 Kings 21:25). People can spiritually "eat things sacrificed to idols," by feeding on false doctrines. Idolatry is spiritual adultery and can involve idolizing people or things. Some people put more emphasis on what the ministers say than on what the Word says. Jeremiah 5:31 states: "The prophets prophesy falsely, and the priest rule by their own power; and My people love to have it so." Rulers were asserting their own authority instead of the authority of the Word, which was something that God said His people loved. Many people today still love to have men ruling over them and admire, highly esteem, and idolize false prophets.

All who are redeemed and delivered from the law are to be bond servants. Romans 6:18 says, "And having been set free from sin, you became slaves (bond servants) of righteousness." Romans 6:22 says, "But now having been set free from sin, and having become slaves of

God, you have your fruit to holiness, and the end, everlasting life." As slaves of God, we are God's purchased possession and property. A bond servant is different than a hired servant because a hired servant does not belong to the master but is only paid to do a task. A bond servant labors for his Lord instead of for money like a hired servant. When Peter addressed the elect—the church—in 1 Peter 2:15–16 he said, "For this is the will of God, that by doing good you may put to silence the ignorance of foolish men as free, yet not using liberty as a cloak for vice, but as bondservants of God." Ephesians 6:6 talks about how even the bond servants of men should be, "but as bond servants of Christ, doing the will of God from the heart." Romans 7:6 says, "we should serve in the newness of the Spirit." It is important to note that this word *serve* literally means to serve as a bond servant, and all the saints have been called to serve in this capacity. In Christianity we serve in the newness of the spirit, but under Judaism the Israelites served in the oldness of the letter.

At the Passover, in John 13:5, Jesus washed the disciples' feet, which would have been a common job of a bond servant in those days. Jesus was setting the example for how the leaders should lead by not putting themselves above others. The apostles did not view what Jesus did as instituting a foot washing ceremony, which is practiced in many of the churches of God. If foot washing was meant to be a new ceremony, then the disciples would have been involved in washing feet also at that time. Foot washing was a common custom that accrued daily at that time when people wore sandals and walked on dirt roads. In John 13:15 Jesus said, "For I have given you an example." This was not a command to have a perfunctory foot-washing ceremony. Many leaders fail to learn the lesson that Jesus taught through His example of washing feet. Jesus demonstrated how leaders are to be as bond servants in serving others.

Some churches of God also have what they call the "anointing cloth," which is not biblical, but the idea came from Acts 19:11–12 where "God did unusual miracles by the hands of Paul." James 5:14 says, "Is anyone among you sick? Let him call for elders of the church, and let them pray over him, anointing him (not a piece of cloth) with oil in the name of the Lord." The important thing to realize is that it is not the anointing of cloth that heals but as James 5: 15 says, "And the prayer of faith will save the sick."

Not all elders are ordained, which means appointed for a certain task, but someone who is older or mature in the faith is an elder, which is what the word *elder* means. Our faith in not directed toward men or in physical things but as Acts 20:21 states: "repentance toward God and faith toward our Lord Jesus Christ." Isaiah 53:4–5 says, "Surely He has borne our griefs and carried our sorrows; Yet we esteemed Him stricken, smitten by God, and afflicted. But He was wounded for our transgressions, He was bruised for our iniquities; The chastisement for our peace was upon Him, and by His stripes we are healed."

11

DOCTRINES OF BALAAM AND NICOLAITANS

The doctrines of the Nicolaitans and Balaam mentioned in the book of Revelation have similarities and can be explained interchangeably. These doctrines were around in the church when John wrote the book of Revelation and will continue to be around in the church even until the day of the Lord's coming (Rev. 1:19). The word *Nicolaitans* means "ruling over the laity" and can also be interpreted as "the conquering of the people."

The deeds and doctrine of the Nicolaitans have to do with corrupt ruling or governance in the church. The deeds and doctrine of the Nicolaitans are things that God hates, according to Revelation 2:15. Knowing that God hates these things should make us diligent to not be involved in them, but if we do not know what these things are then we may be supporting them unintentionally. Ephesians 5:11 says, "and have no fellowship with the unfruitful works of darkness but rather expose them."

Proverbs 6:16–19 mentions six things that God hates. The sixth thing mentioned in Proverbs 6:19 is "a false witness who speaks lies." Proverbs 6:16 states: "Yes, seven are an abomination to Him." The seventh involves not just the sixth but also something else. The seventh would be Proverbs 6:19: "A false witness who speaks lies, and one who sows discord among brethren." John 17:17 says, "God's word is truth." When we speak truth, we do not sow discord, which involves a belief that is unbiblical. Mandating monetary tithes is unbiblical, so those who say that monetary tithing is a biblical requirement are bearing false witness. First John 2:21 says, "no lie is of the truth." John 17:17 says, "Sanctify them by Your truth, Your word is truth." The truth does not change (Mal. 3:6). Today many of the churches of God expect a monetary tithe from those who they perceive as laity. Some in the clergy limit the ministry of church members to pay, pray, and do what they say. Ephesians 4:12 reveals that the saints should be involved in ministry. Ephesians 4:11–12 says, "And He Himself gave some to be apostles, some prophets, some evangelists, and some pastors and teachers for the equipping of the saints for the work of ministry." Members can minister in various ways such as through prayer, music, teaching, giving, and encouraging. The different gifts and abilities that God gives should be for serving, helping, and edifying the church.

The Jewish Christians were addressed in the book of Hebrews 6:10, which says, "For God is not unjust to forget your work and labor of love which you have shown toward His name, in that you have ministered to saints, and do minister." A minister is one who serves. The Hebrews church members were reverting to Judaism, which is why the writer of Hebrews was addressing the reformation or restoring with the new covenant in comparison to the old. First Peter 2:5, 9 refer to all church members under the new covenant as part of a royal priesthood. Those who exercise dominion over other members by requiring monetary tithes to pay themselves are emulating the deeds of the Nicolaitans.

There are various things going on in the church in the end-time that God disapproves. From Revelation 2:1 to Revelation 3:22, God warns the church seven times to repent. God does not want us to be blind to what is going on, which is why we are repeatedly warned throughout the Bible of the massive masquerade of false prophets. First Timothy 4:1–2 states: "Now the Spirit expressly says that in latter times some will depart from the faith, giving heed to deceiving spirits and doctrines of demons, speaking lies in hypocrisy having their own conscience seared with a hot iron." Many ministers are involved in a tithing scam without it even bothering their consciences.

Doctrines that are not according to God's word may fall under the doctrines of demons. One of the doctrines of demons involved "forbidding to marry," according to 1 Timothy 4:3. It has been reported that there are still some pastors among the churches of God who incorrectly teach that brethren of different races are forbidden to marry. Paul was writing to Timothy about things that are going on in the church in this time. The "latter times" mentioned in 1 Timothy 4:3 implies the end of the end-times.

Balaam means "destroyer of the people," and numerous prophesies relate to the destruction caused by false prophets. In Revelation 9:11 Satan is also referred to as Abaddon and Apollyon, which means destruction and destroyer. One of the main ways that Satan destroys is by lies or false doctrines. When John 8:44 talks about the devil it says, "for he is a liar and the father of it." God does not want us to be ignorant of Satan's devices. Ephesians 6:11 says, "Put on the whole armor of God that you may be able to stand against the wiles (scheming) of the devil." Part of the good news is that God's kingdom is "one which shall not be destroyed" (Dan. 2:44, 6:26, 7:14; 2 Pet. 1:11).

Jude talks about ungodly men crept in among God's church. Jude 11 says, "Woe to them! For they have gone in the way of Cain, have run greedily in the error of Balaam for profit, and perish in the rebellion of Korah." The word *Cain* means to get or acquire. The way of Cain is the way of get. False prophets acquire or get false profits. Dishonest gain is part of the ungodly way of Cain. Teaching a false doctrine about tithing is dishonest. Preaching for prestige and pay and abusing authority by requiring money are contributing factors that are indicative of following the way of Balaam.

The error of Balaam was greed and preaching for profit or reward. The word in Jude 11 in the Greek for "profit" also means for pay or hire. Balaam is an example of a prophet that was used by God, but Balaam was also prophesying for pay. Second Peter 2:1–15 reveals that many teachers among God's people are "following the way of Balaam who loved the wages of unrighteousness." A fee was involved in getting Balaam's services (Num. 22:7). Like a harlot, charging a fee for a service connotes selfish motives and serving mammon.

Babylon is the mother of harlots and abominations, according to Revelation 17:5. Hosea 9:1 talks about Israel when it says, "For you have played the harlot against your God. You have made love for hire on every threshing floor." The threshing floor is figurative of the minister's labor (1 Cor. 9:9–10). In Revelation 18:4 when the Word talks about Babylon He says, "Come out of her my people." God's people, meaning the church of God, is admonished to come out of Babylon spiritually speaking. Nehemiah 13:2 mentions how the Ammonites and Moabites hired Balaam. Balaam was a hireling who prophesied for pay. Deuteronomy 23:4 and Jude 11 also corroborate the fact that Balaam was a hireling instead of a bond servant.

Babylon

Mystery Babylon the great, the mother of
harlots and abominations,
has been a negative influence on the earth
for so many generations.
This political and religious system that is so
devoted to materialism,
shall surely be smashed and destroyed for
its corrupt imperialism.
This woman mounted on the beast, full of
names of blasphemy,
shall be punished for her vilification and for
pride and apostasy.
She rejects the true bread of life and labors
for a physical feast,
but there is no rest for anyone who receives
the mark of the beast.
There are the buildings in Babylon that are

constructed with a steeple,
but for those dwelling there, God says, "come
out of her my people."
Doom will come upon this city that was built
with a crooked gate,
because she is filled with confusion and with
demons and with hate.
An end shall come to her sorceries and to the
babbling in Babylon,
and all her merchants, mills, and musicians
will eventually be gone.
Her sins that have reached unto heaven, God
will not forever tolerate,
so she is passing away into perdition and total
ruin shall be her fate.
There are so many whom the beast and false
prophet will mislead,
and desolation shall come to Babylon because
of ignorance and greed.
An antichrist denies the Father and Son and
tries to change their laws,
so this mother is a fake and imitation that is
filled with many flaws.
With the voice of a dragon the beast of Babylon
will issue a decree,
but the saints shall not be duped because the
truth makes them free.
The deception of evil men and seducers will
go from bad to worse,
and all who partake of their pernicious ways
shall be under a curse.
Babylon shall be crushed by the Rock and be
a victim of God's wrath,
and destruction will come upon all who want
to follow in her path.

She was decked with gold, arrayed in purple,
but such a secular city,
being drunken with the blood of the saints on
whom she had no pity.
Babylon is a wicked world that is so deceived
by the father of lies,
and so there is nothing panegyrical about what
Babylon implies.
This scarlet-colored beast with the seven heads
and ten horns,
shall be judged by the true King, the One they
crowned with thorns.
The fierce anger of God shall come, and heaven
and earth shall shake,
and the nations will be broken into pieces for
the law that they break.
We can see the rise and fall of Babylon from
an exegetical view,
with plagues of death, mourning, and famine
for being so untrue.
The saints shall rule with Christ the King who
expels the evil empire,
because the saints worship the true God who
saves them from the fire.
There will be a complete annihilation of this
mother, the great Babylon,
and then there will be peace on earth, where
God's will is to be done.

Your kingdom come, Your will be done on
earth as it is in heaven. (Matthew 6:10)

In John chapter 10, Jesus is addressing corrupt religious leaders who climb up some other way and not the way Jesus exemplified while being a bond servant. False leaders are referred to as thieves and robbers (John 10:1). In John 10:12–13, while Jesus is still addressing the religious leaders, He reveals how the hireling flees when danger comes. John 10:13 says, "The hireling flees because he is a hireling and does not care about the sheep." The hireling is more concerned about protecting himself than the sheep. The hireling may be more concerned about the pay than the people. The hireling can be just serving mammon and himself at the expense of others since he flees in times of danger.

Romans 16:18 is talking about those who cause divisions with a contradictory doctrine. Making changes to God's tithing laws would be contrary to God's word. Romans 16:18 says, "For those who are such do not serve our Lord Jesus Christ, but their own belly, and by smooth words and flattering speech deceive the hearts of the simple." Many false prophets are smooth talkers or good speakers, which is one of the ways that they deceive people. Enforcing a tithe on members is the same as charging a fee for a service, which is not something that a true bond servant of Jesus should do. Titus 1:10–11 talks about deceivers who destroy or subvert, "teaching things which they ought not, for the sake of dishonest gain." These things involve the commandments of men. Mandating monetary tithing is a commandment of men.

Jude 11 reveals that Korah's rebellion is still going on today among God's people. Korah's rebellion involved leaders—"men of renown"—highly esteemed among the congregation, according to Numbers 16:2, who desired a priesthood that God did not establish for them. Under the new covenant all members of the body of Christ are a part of the holy and royal priesthood (1 Pet. 2:5, 9). Those who put themselves in a position where they take tithes, which God did not appoint for them, are involved in the modern gainsaying of Korah. Korah's rebellion involved trying to change what God ordained for the Levitical priesthood. Korah's rebellion influenced all the congregation to go against Moses and Aaron (Num. 16:41–42). When we change what God instructed for Moses and Aaron, including the tithing laws, then we are not just going against Moses and Aaron, but we are also going against the Word of God.

The deeds of the Nicolaitans implicate the conquering of the people. Throughout the Bible whenever a nation was conquered and ruled over by another nation, the survivors of the conquered people were put under tribute. Judges 1:28–33; Joshua 16:10, 17:13; 2 Kings 23:33, 23:35; and 1 Kings 4:21 are some examples of how tribute was imposed on the conquered people. Tribute is a forced payment or tax placed on those who are considered subordinate. The Jews were required to pay taxes to the Romans because they were under the subjugation of its empire. Revelation 6:2 talks about a false prophet who "went out conquering and to conquer," so people came under his subjugation.

Gentile kings exercised dominion and took tribute, tithes, or taxes from the people to support their lucrative lifestyles and to recompense their officers, army, and hired servants. When Israel rejected God as their King and wanted a human king to reign over them like the Gentile nations, they were warned that their kings would also do like the Gentile kings and take a tenth of their possessions as mentioned in 1 Samuel 8:15. The Israelites not only paid a tithe to the Levites but also paid a tithe or additional tax to their human kings who ruled over them.

Many preachers persuade members to serve them by requiring them to pay for their houses, cars, clothes, food, and whole livelihood through distorting what the Word teaches on tithing. Those who coerce tithes to support their copious lifestyles are certainly being served by members whom they exercise authority over. Brethren who have been duped by a lie and the false doctrine on tithing are paying for this deception. Psalm 40:4 says, "Blessed is that man who makes the Lord his trust, And does not respect the proud, nor such as turn aside to lies." The doctrine of the Nicolaitans, or ruling over the laity, was not supported by the foundation of the apostles, prophets, and Jesus Christ the chief cornerstone.

The cornerstone is the preeminent part of the foundation that supports the rest of the building. Matthew 21:44 says, "And whoever falls on this stone will be broken, but on whomever it falls, it will grind him to powder." Some fall on the stone because of apathy, or a lack of interest, zeal, or passion. The stone will pulverize some because of their enmity and malevolence. We need to stick to the stone that many reject and stumble over. Isaiah 28:16 says, "Therefore thus says the Lord God; Behold, I lay in Zion a stone for a foundation, A tried stone, a precious cornerstone, a sure foundation; Whoever believes will not act hastily." We need to think things over before we act to make sure our actions are according to the Word. When we act according to the Word then we have God's support.

Jesus was asked about paying the temple tax in Matthew 17: 24–27. Jesus asked Simon in verse 25, "From whom do the kings of the earth take customs or taxes from, sons or strangers?" Peter said, "from strangers." The strangers were the conquered or subordinate people. Then Jesus said, "then the sons are free." Even the pagan kings did not tax their own family. First Samuel 17:25 talks about the one who kills Goliath will be given the king's daughter. He would be treated as family and be exempt from paying taxes in Israel. Under the old covenant the priesthood was exempt from paying a temple tax since they belonged to God and were not numbered among the people.

In Matthew 17:24–27 our King Jesus was making the point that the sons of God are not strangers but belong to God's royal household (Eph. 2:19). Freedom was declared by Jesus for the sons of the God. This freedom included freedom from the legalism of being taxed under the law. The gospel of the kingdom of God is about a spiritual incorruptible kingdom (1 Cor. 15:50). The word *kingdom* is derived from the words *king's dominion*. Under God's ascendancy, the sons of God are not taxed. The sons of God are those who receive the Holy Spirit and worship God in truth and spirit and not just in a physical temple.

The Problem with Pay

The hiring of priests in the Bible was originally associated with idolatry and spiritual adultery. This occurred during the time when "there was no king in Israel and everyone did what was right in his own eyes" (Judg. 17:6). Jonathan, the son of Gershom, the son of Moses, was an apostate Levite hired by a man named Micah.

Money was made into idols and brought into the house of Micah where the Levite was hired to serve as a priest (Judg. 17:10, 18:4). This idolatrous priestly service continued on through the tribe of Dan (Judg. 18:19–20).The hiring of a priestly ministry among Israel was not sanctioned by God's law. Micah means "who is like Jehovah." The house of Micah was a counterfeit house that tried to appear like the house of God (Judg. 17:1–13). The house of Micah is still around today under different names.

The book of Micah addresses the syncretism of Samaria, which symbolizes an impure religion. A different Micah from the one in Judges was falsely accused of prattle or babbling, according to Micah 2:6. Micah warns about lying prophets whose message was inconsistent with the Word. Micah 3:5 states: "Thus says the Lord concerning the prophets who make my people stray, who chant peace, while they chew with their teeth." This verse literally means (who chant all is well for those who feed them).

The second part of Micah 3:5 expresses the motives of false prophets who cannot get your financial support. Micah 3:5 continues saying, "But who prepare war against him who puts nothing into their mouths." False prophets prey on people and feed themselves at the expense of others. Some of these preachers may even become inimical toward those who will not comply with supporting them in their iniquity.

Micah 3:8 states how Micah was "full of power by the Spirit of the Lord, to declare to Israel his sin." Micah 3:9–11 is also a prophetic message for spiritual Israel, which is the church today. "Now hear this, You heads of the house of Jacob and rulers of the house of Israel, who abhor justice and pervert all equity (fairness), Who build up Zion (symbolic of the church) with bloodshed (atrocities) and Jerusalem with iniquity." Micah 3:11 says, "Her heads judge for bribe, Her priests (chief rulers) teach for pay, and her prophets divine for money, Yet they lean on the Lord, and say, is not the Lord among us?" These rulers among God's people were deceiving themselves, saying "is not the Lord among us?" while they preached for pay.

Under the old covenant, the Levites received agrarian tithes for their service. The prophets were given gifts of gratitude for their service, but corrupt prophets like Balaam and soothsayers charged a fee and were paid for their service (Num. 22:7). Numbers 24:1 also reveals that Balaam was involved at times in fortune-telling or sorcery. In 2 Kings 5:15–20 Elisha chose not to accept the gifts of Naaman for his service, but Gehazi the servant of Elisha pursued after these things and was cursed with leprosy. The example in the old covenant of God's prophets shows that they were offered gifts like in 2 Kings 8:8 or 1 Samuel 9:7. The true prophets were not paid for using their gift in the service of God.

One of the problems of receiving pay for serving the Lord is that it can become a bribe or subversion. The hireling may be more motivated by the love of money than by the love of the Lord. Those who are being paid often have a propensity to please the one who is providing the pay. Exodus 23:8 states: "And you shall take no bribe, for a bribe blinds the discerning and perverts the words of the righteous." Deuteronomy 16:19 states: "You shall not pervert justice; you shall not show partiality, nor take a bribe, for a bribe blinds the eyes of the wise and twists the words of the righteous." Being paid or bribed can influence one's arbitration on certain matters. If a minister knows that his income is coming from the tithes of members, then he may be a little partial or blind to the fact that the Bible does not enforce nor endorse mandatory monetary tithing.

We should realize that history repeats itself. Second Peter 2:1 states: "But there were also false prophets among the people, even as there will be false teachers among you." Among physical Israel there were many false prophets and corrupt leaders, and this is also a reality today among the church. Isaiah 1:23 says, "Your princes (rulers) are rebellious, and companions of thieves; Everyone loves bribes, And follows after rewards" (payoffs).

Isaiah 9:15–16 says, "The prophet who teaches lies he is the tail. For the leaders of this people cause them to err, and those who are led by them are destroyed." During the time of Judges, we have the example of how the sons of Samuel allowed bribes to corrupt them. First Samuel 8:3 says, "But his sons did not walk in his ways; they turned aside after dishonest gain, took bribes, and perverted justice." The acquiring of dishonest gain was a part of the iniquity in the past among Israel and continues to be a part of the iniquity abounding in this end-time (Matt. 24:11–12).

There are many warnings for us in both the Old and New Testament about false prophets, but few seem to realize the magnitude of it among God's people because it is covered up in a masquerade of righteousness. Jude talks about those among God's people who go the way of Cain, Balaam, and Korah, who are referred to in Jude 12 as "spots in your love feasts." The word *spots* literally means "hidden reefs." These spots, stains, or blemishes are hidden among God's people in sheep's clothing, disguised with the appearance of righteousness.

There are artificial or superficial lights among the light that gives light (Matt. 5:15). Second Corinthians 11:14 says, "And no wonder! For Satan himself transforms himself into an angel of light." Paul chose not to accept financial support to expose false apostles who sought money for their services. Those who sought money for preaching the gospel were described as "false apostles and deceitful workers, transforming (disguising) themselves into apostles of Christ (2 Cor. 11:7–13).

Greed, preaching for money, and preeminence are characteristics of deceitful workers. Jeremiah 5:26 says, "For among My people are found wicked men." Jeremiah 5:27–28 says, "So their houses are full of deceit therefore they have become great and grown rich. They have grown fat, they are sleek." These false prophets were well fed and groomed; they made sure that they took care of themselves. Jeremiah 5:28 says, "They do not plead the cause, the cause of the fatherless; Yet they (false prophets) prosper, and the right of the needy they do not defend." Isaiah 1:16 is an admonition for Israel to repent. Isaiah 1:17 says, "Learn to do good; Seek justice, Rebuke the oppressor; Defend the fatherless. Plead for the widow." Proverbs 31:9 says, "Open your mouth, judge righteously, and plead the cause of the poor and needy." Within the church of God organizations even the needy are expected to paid tithes to support a ministry that is sleek, well paid, and prosperous. False teachings on tithing have brought about expropriation and wealth for corrupt ministers. God was not pleased with many of the leaders among physical Israel, and the warnings for them are also for the leaders in the church today. In Zechariah 10:3 God says, "My anger is kindled against the shepherds (pastors), And I will punish the goatherds (leaders)." Zechariah 13:3 talks about false prophets that have "spoken lies in the name of the Lord." Isaiah refers to the leaders or shepherds as being greedy dogs.

Isaiah 55:11 says, "Yes they are greedy dogs which never have enough. And they are shepherds who cannot understand; They all look to their own way, Every one for his own gain." Philippians 3:2 states: "Beware of dogs, beware of evil workers, beware of the mutilation!" Paul was addressing those who were Judaizers as dogs. These people were trying to enforce old covenant ordinances including physical circumcision on the Philippians.

Peter concludes his comments about false teachers among God's people in 2 Peter 2:22, which says, "But it has happened to them according to the true proverb: "A dog returns to his own vomit." Dogs can refer to those who were prostituting by peddling the word of God. Dogs are among those who are excluded from the New Jerusalem. Revelation 22:15 says, "But outside are dogs and sorcerers and sexually immoral and murderers and idolaters, and whoever loves and practices a lie." There are many who teach a lie about what the Word says on tithing.

Colossians 2:8 says, "Beware least anyone cheat you through philosophy and empty deceit, according to the tradition of men, according to the basic principles of the world, and not according to Christ." The words "cheat you" literally mean to plunder you or take you captive, which involved making people pay tribute to them. The taxing of laity is a tradition of men and a basis principle of the world that has become a part of a crooked administration within the church.

Colossians 2:8 warns us to not be cheated by teachings that are not according to Christ the Word. The doctrine of mandating monetary tithes to paid preachers is not according to the Word and does not concur with Ephesians 6:3: "the words of our Lord Jesus Christ and to the doctrine which accords with godliness." Jesus never told His disciples to collect monetary tithes from members of the church or from anyone and use it to pay themselves a nice salary. Jude 4 warns us about how Satan's counterfeits have crept in unnoticed among the church and pervert God's grace.

The ministers that Jesus first sent out to preach the gospel of the kingdom of God were told in Matthew 10:9 to "provide neither gold nor silver nor copper in your money belts." One of the first lessons that they were to learn was that they were not to minister for their own personal profit. The twelve were to trust in God to provide their needs, and they were to allow the beneficiaries of their ministry to share with them. The early disciples were essentially told to take what was needed (Matt. 10:10) and avoid greed. Toward the end of Christ's earthly ministry, in Luke 22:36, Jesus also instructed the disciples to use normal means such as buying and selling to obtain their needs.

Wolves among the Sheep

The term *wolves* applies to false prophets. Matthew 7:15 states: "Beware of false prophets, who come to you in sheep's clothing but inwardly they are ravenous wolves." Sheep's clothing implies the clothing of a shepherd. In Matthew 10:16 Jesus said, "Behold I send you out as sheep in the midst of wolves." Wolves are the rapacious false prophets that plunder the sheep. The wolves in sheep's clothing appear to be ministers of righteousness, but these deceitful workers are involved in getting dishonest gain. The wolves want to feed themselves by preying on the sheep for money. This is also a reason why Paul emphasized so much that bishops and deacons are not to be lovers of money, which at that time came from the donations of those who were being taught the Word.

It was common in the early church just as it is today to have wolves among God's sheep. In Acts 20:29–30 Paul said, "For I know this, that after my departure savage wolves will come in among you, (God's people) not sparing the flock. Also from among yourselves men will rise up, speaking perverse things, to draw away the disciples after themselves." One reason we have divisions among God's church is because men draw away the disciples after themselves. Acts 20:30 tells us that from among God's people some will be "speaking perverse things." The misleading things spoken in the church include the doctrines of the Nicolaitans and Balaam (Rev. 2:14–15).

Another reason for divisions among God's people is carnality. First Corinthians 3:3 says, "for you are still carnal. For where there are envy, strife, and divisions among you, are you not carnal and behaving like mere men?" Christians should not behave like mere men walking in worldly ways. Carnality is a lack of true spirituality, and carnality reflects immaturity in Christ as 1 Corinthians 3:1 refers to the carnal as being "babes in Christ." God wants us to go beyond the milk and take in the solid food of His word. Hebrews 5:13 reveals that if we partake only of milk then we are still "a babe." As we mature, we can take in the solid food of the Word (Heb. 5:14).

Ezekiel was a priest and in the Babylonian captivity with the nation of Judah when he wrote his warning for Judah and Israel. The northern house of Israel had already been taken into captivity and was removed from their land of Samaria, so this warning of Ezekiel never reached the nation of Israel. This confirms that these warnings are also for spiritual Israel being God's church today. Ezekiel 22:25–27 states: "The conspiracy of her prophets in her midst is like a roaring lion tearing the prey; they have devoured people they have taken treasure and precious things; they have made many widows in her midst. Her priests have violated My law like wolves tearing the prey, to shed blood, to destroy people, and get dishonest gain." Ezekiel 22:25–27 is a warning for us today about rulers among God's church who are involved in this conspiracy to get dishonest gain.

Zephaniah also warns about the leadership among God's people. Zephaniah 3:3–4 says, "Her princes in her midst are roaring lions; Her judges are evening wolves that leave not a bone till morning. Her prophets are insolent treacherous people; Her priests have polluted the sanctuary, They have done violence to the law." The religious leaders violated or mistreated the law by not applying it correctly.

First Peter 1:10–12, 2 Peter 1:19–21, and 2 Peter 2:1, along with other scriptures verify that we need to be aware of what the prophets wrote.

First Peter 5:2–3 talks about shepherding the flock but not for dishonest gain. Not being honest about what the Word says about tithing is a way to get dishonest gain. Ezekiel 22:28 talks about prophets divining lies, saying, "thus says the Lord God, when the Lord has not spoken." How many preachers have falsely said or implied that "the Word (the Lord) says you must tithe money to the church," even though the Word does not say that? If you cannot prove that the tithing of money is scriptural, then you cannot truthfully say "thus says the Lord God" when the Lord has not spoken it. No one can truthfully say, "it is written, thou shall tithe money" when the Word does not state that.

Ahab and Zedekiah prophesized a lie in God's name and were delivered into the hand of Nebuchadnezzar, king of Babylon. This example should help us to realize the seriousness of this misconduct. God allowed Ahab and Zedekiah to be "roasted in the fire" by the king for committing adultery and for speaking lying words in God's name, which God had not commanded (Jer. 29:21–23). Colossians 3:17 says, "and whatever you do in word or deed, do all in the name of the Lord Jesus, giving thanks to God the Father through Him." When we do and say things in the name of Jesus, we do and say things by His authority. When we say things that are not according to the Word, then it is not something that we are honestly doing or saying in the name of our Lord.

12

THE GOVERNANCE JESUS SANCTIONED

The kingdom that Jesus taught His apostles was the opposite of man's government. Jesus explains what He authorized for His followers in Luke 22:25–27: "And He said to them, 'The kings of the Gentiles exercise lordship over them, and those who exercise authority over them are called benefactors,' But not so among you; on the contrary, he who is greatest among you, let him be as the younger, and he who governs as he who serves." Gentile kings exercised lordship over the subjugated people, which involved collecting taxes or tribute or tithes from the people. In Luke 22:26 Jesus said, "But not so among you; on the contrary." God's administration is contrary to man's government.

Jesus said in Luke 22:25: "those who exercise authority over them are called benefactors." A benefactor is one who gives benefits like a king from taking taxes. First Samuel 8:15 says, "He (the king) will take a tenth of your grain and your vintage, and give it to his officers and servants." Many churches of God enforce the paying of tithes where one person is the chief and benefactor who pays or gives benefits to pastors serving under his authority. The autocracy set up in many of the churches of God allows whoever is in charge to choose how much he pays himself and those working under him. The only limit is based on the amount of money taken in.

Gentile kings exercised authority over people by having control over the taxes they imposed. Jesus went on to say in Luke 22:26: "He who is greatest among you, let him be as the younger, and he who governs as he who serves." First Peter 5:5 mentions that the younger are to submit to their elders. In Ephesians 5:21 Paul was addressing the whole church when he wrote, "submitting to one another in the fear of God." After this admonition then specific instructions are given for wives, husbands, children, bond servants, and masters (Eph. 5:22–6:9). In Luke 22:27 Jesus used His own example and said, "I am among you as One who serves," and we see that Jesus served as a bond servant instead of a hired servant (Phil. 2:7).

Mark 10:42–45 also records this message of Jesus for those who want to be the chief rulers: they are to be servants. Mark 10:44 says, "and whoever of you desires to be first (chief) shall be slave (bond servant) of all. A slave or bond servant did not work for pay. Mark 10:45 states: "For the Son of man did not come to be served, but to serve, and to give His life a ransom for many." Many ministers coerce members to serve them by mandating tithes.

Jesus gave His life as a ransom that paid the price to release us from bondage, and our Lord offers us liberty (Gal. 5:11–13). Religious leaders who try to enforce old covenant ordinances and the commandments of men may want to keep you in bondage or under their control. Galatians 4:9 states: "But now after you have known God, or rather are known by God, how is it that you turn again to the weak and beggarly elements, to which you desire again to be in bondage?" These elements involved both Jewish religious ordinances and Gentile traditions.

Paul uses sarcasm at times, which may make some of what he writes harder to understand if you are not aware of that. Second Corinthians 11:19 says, "For you put up with fools gladly, since you yourselves are wise!" The fools are the blind religious leaders, who Jesus also addressed as fools in Matthew 23. Fools are those who fool people including themselves. After Paul warns about these false apostles and deceitful workers, he went on to say how the Corinthians accepted them.

Many brethren today are just like the Corinthians in Paul's day. Second Corinthians 11:20 says, "for you put up with it, (allow it) if one brings you into bondage, (old covenant edicts) if one devours you (like a wolf), if one takes from you (extorting money), if one exalts himself" (lords over), if one strikes you on the face (disrespects you). Paul was talking about what the false ministers were doing among God's church and how the brethren were gladly accepting or allowing it; sadly this is still going on today among the church.

In 2 Corinthians 11:20, Paul used the words "if one devours you," which involves corrupt teachers preying upon members for financial support. The word *devour* is the same verb used in Mark. 12:38–40 and Luke 20:47 where Jesus criticized the religious leaders for devouring widows' houses, whom they took advantage of for their own financial gain. First Peter 5:8 says, "Be sober, be vigilant; because your adversary the devil walks about like a roaring lion, seeking whom he may devour." The Corinthians, just like many today, were not watchful and aware of the corruption going on in the ministry among the church. Matthew 20:25–28 also expounds on how God's government is not like man's where often the weak support the strong. In God's way the strong are to support the weak as mentioned in Romans 15:1. In Acts 20:35 Paul said, "I have shown you in every way, by laboring like this, that you must support the weak." The poor and weak among us should receive support by those who are able to freely give, as Paul reiterated in 2 Corinthians 9:1–14 and other scriptures. Jesus taught that the greatest among us were to serve and not to be served by ruling over people like the rulers of the Gentiles. One of the ways the worldly governments ruled over people was by requiring taxes, tribute, or tithes.

Ministers who enforce monetary tithes to get paid are exercising authority that has not been given to them by the head of the body, which is Jesus. Making people pay contrary to the Word can be a matter of oppression, domination, and subjugation. The governance that Jesus implemented for the church did not involve the worldly customs of leaders exercising dominion over people. Matthew 20:25–26 says, "But Jesus called them to Himself and said, You know that the rulers of the Gentiles lord it over them, and those who are great exercise authority over them. Yet it shall not be so among you; but whoever desires to become great among you, let him be your servant. And whoever desires to be first among you, let him be your slave." Slaves were not like the hirelings who worked for pay.

The way church leaders are to exercise authority should not involve mandating a 10 percent tax from the members. Those who "lord over" are putting themselves in a category over or above other church members. The church is one body with just one head, being Jesus (Eph. 5:23). Those who esteem themselves above others may fail to understand the leadership of serving as a slave or bond servant. Humility is required to be great in the kingdom.

Matthew 23:11–12 says, "but he who is greatest among you shall be your servant. And whoever exalts himself will be humbled, and he who humbles himself will be exalted." Leaders should lead in applying what Paul said in Philippians 2:3–4: "Let nothing be done through selfish ambition or conceit, but in lowliness of mind let each esteem others better than himself. Let each of you look out not only for his own interests, but also for the interests of others." What many preachers falsely teach about tithing is not for the interests of others but for their own self-interests.

CONCLUSION

Those who labor for our Lord have the right to receive support. This support can come in various ways and not just financially.

Jesus said, "The laborer is worthy of his wages." These wages involved lodging ministers and providing food and drink (Luke 10:7). The new covenant exhorts fellowshipping or sharing. There is no legalistic obligation to pay monetary tithes when we freely give. Matthew 10:8 says, "Freely you have received, freely give." It pleases God when we share instead of being forced to pay a certain percent (Heb. 13:16).

When it comes to God's word on tithing, we can either believe that the Bible means what it says and says what it means, or we can believe whatever men choose to change about the tithing laws to serve and benefit themselves with dishonest gain. It is imperative that we give more credence to what the word of God says than what humans say. The word of God says to tithe agrarian products, crops, fruits from the trees, and specific farm animals (Deut. 14:22, Lev. 27:30–32). Humans say to tithe money. Do you believe the word of God or do you believe the teachings of humans?

The word of God states that the Levites have a command to receive (agrarian) tithes from the people as an inheritance according to the law (Heb. 7:5, Num. 18:26). We cannot repudiate the fact that Jesus did not come to change the law (Matt. 5:17–19, Luke 16:17). Humans teach maybe even inadvertently that they can change God's laws on tithing by teaching that non-Levites are now entitled to receive monetary tithes. Do you believe the word of God, or do you believe the teachings of humans?

Various scriptures confirm that the Spirit-led Christians are not under the letter of the law with the Levitical priesthood (Gal. 5:18, Rom. 7:6). The word of God teaches under the new covenant to freely give, and Paul reiterates this by saying, "give as he purposes in his heart, not grudgingly or of necessity" or compulsion (2 Cor. 9:7). Jesus taught that the giver determines the amount that he chooses to give (Luke 6:38). Men say that brethren are required by law to pay monetary tithes. Do you believe the word of God or do you believe the teachings of humans?

John 8:32 says, "and you shall know the truth, and the truth shall make you free." John 8:36 says, "therefore if the Son makes you free, you shall be free indeed." Christ is our King, and we are Christ's, who was as Galatians 4:5 states: "born under the law, to redeem those who were under the law, that we might receive the adoption as sons. And because you are sons, God has sent forth the Spirit of His Son into your hearts, crying out Abba, Father." Our Redeemer and King has freed us from the yoke of bondage (Rom. 8:15). God has given us His Spirit and has made us a part of His holy family "and if children, then heirs—heirs of God and join theirs with Christ" (Rom. 8:14–17).

Our Father loved us so much that He sacrificed His Son, and Jesus paid the penalty for our sins. Our compassionate God and Jesus loved us so much that they were willing to suffer for us. Romans 8:32 says, "He who did not spare His own Son, but delivered Him up for us all, how shall He not with Him also freely give us all things?" The abundant life that God wants to freely give us is the life of Christ, which God is sharing with us now. Colossians 3:4 says, "When Christ who is our life appears, then you also will appear with Him in glory." Galatians 5:1 says, "Stand fast therefore in the liberty by which Christ has made us free, and do not be entangled again with a yoke of bondage." Let's be thankful for the love, liberty, and life of our Lord Jesus, which is freely given to us in Christ.

The Word

With the Word of God we will progress
without turning back,
so we must press toward the goal for the
prize and stay on track,
and the Word is a mighty weapon we use
against Satan's attack,
since our adversary wants to hit us with
more than just a smack,
but we have a great God who heals us and
not just some quack,
and the Word is a sword that can circumcise
a heart with a hack,
and from the Holy Spirit we can also have
a godly gift or knack,
and the Word of life is our Jesus the loving
leader of our pack,
so we will boldly preach the Word and not
just gibber and yak,
because the Word of truth is in us and not
just in a book on rack,
and the Word is a special treasure that
comes from an endless stack,
for the Word is more valuable than gold and
silver stuffed in a sack,
and the Word is our foundation that will
never break or crack,
and the Word prepares for us a mansion
and not just a shack,
and the Word provides for us a feast and
not just some snack,

for the Word is spiritual food and far better
than any big Mac,
and the Word gives a reward far greater
than any trophy or plaque,
and the Word is the way out of a world
that is out of whack,
and the Word is a light that can brighten
the bleakness of the black,
and the Word can really lift us up so we
can use it like a jack,
and in the awesome power of the Word
there will never be a lack,
so we must live by the Word of our God
without being slack.

Blessed are those who hear the word of
God and keep it. (Luke 11:28)

Printed in the United States
By Bookmasters